KIDS AT THE D

The Practice of Social Work

General editors: Bill Jordan and Jean Packman

Kids at the Door

A Preventive Project on a Council
Estate

BOB HOLMAN

with DAVE WILES and SANDIE LEWIS

Basil Blackwell · Oxford

First published in 1981 by
Basil Blackwell Publisher
108 Cowley Road
Oxford OX4 1JF
England

British Library Cataloguing in Publication Data

Holman, Bob, b.1936
    Kids at the door. — (Practice of social work).
    1. Child welfare
    I. Title   II. Wiles, Dave   III. Lewis, Sandie
    IV. Series

    ISBN 0-631-12586-8
    ISBN 0-631-12587-6 Pbk

Typesetting by Cambrian Typesetters, Farnborough
Printed in Great Britain by
Book Plan, Worcester

Contents

To my sister, Janet

Preface

An account of three years in the life of a community child care project is not intended as an academic treatise. It has had to be composed on the job, so rarely, if ever, have I written for an uninterrupted hour. Despite the obvious deficiencies, I hope the book portrays the scope, the atmosphere, the advantages and disadvantages of child care in the community. Others may decide that to pursue similar projects is a worthwhile objective.

The book has been written with the knowledge and co-operation of local people. Their contributions were invited and a competition was held for the title. None the less, Edgetown is not the real name of the estate. The names of residents and, at times, certain facts about their circumstances have been changed. The reason is that identification might encourage others to come and 'look at' Edgetown or even to label it a 'problem area'. It deserves no such title for, as I explained, Edgetown is an ordinary council estate.

My thanks are due to so many people. To my colleague and close friend, Dave Wiles, whose ideas and actions are so much a part of this book that he must be regarded as a co-author. To Donna Wiles who must think she married the project as well as Dave. To Jane Thomas and Tim Tappenden who tried to persuade me to spend more time writing. To many colleagues in the Church of England Children's Society who backed the project in so many ways. Needless to say, the views expressed are mine and not necessarily those of the Society. To Ian Plaister and Hugh Trenchard for supplying statistical material and David Barker for some wise guidance. To Bill Jordan, the editor of this series who also drew the pictures that grace the book. To Richard Mills who became more than an official of the Calouste Gulbenkian Foundation and helped by always demonstrating that he had faith in what we were doing. To Audrey Browne who undertook all the typing, corrected my spelling errors and never lost her cool when chiding 'Mr Forgetful', as she called me. To my wife Annette, my daughter Ruth and son David whose tolerance, support and love is more than I deserve. And to all the residents of Edgetown with whom I am now linked as a neighbour and friend.

1 The Beginning

'A man turned up'

> I have lived in Edgetown for 13 years and ever since I have been
> at Edgetown there has been quite a lot of vandalism and stealing.
> Then about three years ago, a man turned up . . . .

So wrote a young teenager looking back at the Edgetown
Community Project. When he put pen to paper the project
was well established locally and he had become closely associated with it. But in the beginning that man felt very unsure
of himself.

FROM COLLEGE TO COMMUNITY

I was that man who turned up. What made me come? For
some years I had been a university lecturer and professor with a
particular interest in delinquents and children taken into public
care. My studies showed me that in general taking youngsters
away from their homes was not a beneficial course of action.
For instance, it is known that of boys released from approved
schools, some two-thirds are reconvicted within three years.
Reconviction rates for detention centres and borstals are even
higher.[1] Even if the youngsters have not committed an offence,
there is no certainty that they can be found satisfactory foster
homes or children's homes. I was convinced that the best
approach was to try to *prevent* children becoming delinquent
or having to be separated from their families.

Local authority Social Services Departments have the
powers to do preventive work. Much as I admire the work of
the council social workers, I concluded that their preventive

actions were limited by several factors. Often they carried large and mixed caseloads which included the elderly, the mentally disordered, the disabled and chronically sick as well as families in need of help. Consequently, they could not concentrate on youngsters who might get into trouble. Further, the size of their caseloads and of the areas they covered meant that people could not be seen as regularly or as frequently as was necessary. Most important, social workers tended not to live in the localities where they worked. Even their offices might be some miles from the people most in need of help. It followed that social workers could know closely neither the people nor the neighbourhoods where preventive work was needed. Prevention, I decided, would be more effectively pursued by someone who could concentrate on it and who lived in or near the locality where they worked.

Simultaneously, I was dissatisfied with academic life. Although teaching and writing were enjoyable, administration was not. In particular, endless committee meetings with long speeches about points of order or the definition of terms frustrated me beyond endurance. Moreover, I had little appetite for the internal power battles, the obsession with expanding departmental boundaries and the overwhelming concern with status. In short, I was not much good at the job.

The growing desire to move out of the university was reinforced by a long-felt nagging inner voice telling me to practise again as a social worker. The voice, no doubt, stemmed from certain political and Christian beliefs which, for some years, I had tried to relate to my everyday life. They led me to conclude that my talents, such as they were, should be used amongst people with greater social needs than university personnel. In addition, I believed that the affluence of a professor's life-style was inconsistent with Christian teaching on sharing.

Thus the combination of the above factors led to the decision to jack-in the university gown and to seek a role in preventive social work.

THE PROJECT IDEA

Gradually, the idea of a community child care project crystallized in my mind. In order to maximize the chances of effective prevention, I reckoned that a project needed the following ingredients:

A readiness to use any kind of social work skills. The worker could not confine himself to one of the traditional approaches of social work—casework, group work or community work—but would have to use whatever approach seemed appropriate.
A willingness to live near the place of work in order that the worker should both be readily available to local people and be more able to understand the needs and strengths of the locality.
A concentration on family and child care issues so that the worker's time was not spread too thinly over a wide variety of difficulties.

For shorthand, the above combination is called community social work. The aims of the project became narrowed to:

1 Trying to keep children from being taken into public care.
2 Attempting to help delinquents.
3 Providing some youth amenities for an estate which had hardly any.[2]

Thus, the aims and methods of a community approach were worked out and I was willing to back my ideas by doing the job. The next problem was to raise some money. Two charitable trusts agreed to finance the project for three years, but argued that it should be administratively under the umbrella of a larger agency. The Church of England Children's Society agreed to take the project on board. This step, which only happened because of a fortuitous meeting, proved a happy one. I welcomed the opportunity to work for a Christian organization. The Society's officers were enthusiastic about the aims and methods and also gave me the independence and flexibility needed to develop a community initiative. By the autumn of 1976 I was ready to leave college and commence work on a council estate which can be referred to as Edgetown.

WHY EDGETOWN?

Edgetown and its surrounding district spread across two former wards.[3] Why was it decided to locate the project here? Firstly, figures indicated Edgetown to be an area where youngsters were more likely to be separated from their families. For instance, in 1976, of all the juvenile offenders in the city's 15 wards, 38 per cent came from these two wards. The Social Services Department were of the opinion that a high proportion of their referrals originated from Edgetown. Figures show that Edgetown consistently rates second and third in the league table of new cases referred to the Social Services Department. The comprehensive school in Edgetown referred children at well over twice the rate of any other school in the city. In a 34-month period, it drew attention to over 330 children. Vandalism was reported in the area. Indeed, one house was so damaged that the council found it cheaper to demolish than to spend £12,000 on repairs. Secondly, the estate was marked by a lack of amenities or voluntary groups. Thirdly, and importantly, I already knew some people on the estate and had discussed the possibility of the project with them. Thus, not only was the need apparent, but so, too, was the knowledge that at least a few residents would welcome the project.

What is Edgetown like? Its core is a council estate built in the inter-war years. At one end it merges into more modern local authority buildings. The area also contains modern private dwellings, mostly at the cheaper end of the market, as well as some Victorian artisan buildings. In appearance, it is not unpleasant. The buildings have a mellow look while, being on the outskirts of the city, the estate overlooks green countryside. The pavements, winding and twisty, are broken up by strips of what were once grass, but is now mostly mud. Many of the pre-war council houses have been subjected to a modernization programme. This ran into difficulties partly because the modernization led to condensation and increased dampness in some homes and partly because the council did not have sufficient money to finish fences and gates. Both issues received press publicity when mothers complained about the adverse effects on their children's health and safety. Further, the wards do have some overcrowding and the artisan dwellings lack basic amenities. However, the area could not be said to have poor housing conditions. Its lacks are in other directions.

A local councillor writes, 'Edgetown grew up between the two world wars and like so much of the city's development it lacked imagination in planning and social amenities.'[4] What amenities are there? A large comprehensive boys' school. A junior school, which has received much publicity because of a long-standing leaking roof and an infants school. Two pubs and a working man's club. Four churches of which only one has a minister. Some playgroups. But the estate has only one shop, no cafe, no fish-and-chip shop. No bank. No football pitches. No day nursery or nursery school. Nothing for the elderly. No community buildings. No youth facilities. Three miles from the city centre, residents face an expensive journey on the bus in order to reach large shops, the sports complex or the hospital. The isolation is underlined by the low proportion of people with access to a car in proportion to the rest of the city. Hence people must use the buses, but the return fare for a family of four to the city is over £2. There is a local joke that only the rich can afford to visit the social security offices.

Edgetown is not an unusual council estate. It may well be typical of hundreds of others. My hope was that if the project worked here, it would work elsewhere.

THE START

'How do your start?' I woke up that autumnal morning in 1976 wondering what I had done. The project could hardly be more tin-pot. True, my family had moved into a suitable house alongside the estate. Once the local doctor's house, its old, large rooms would be ideal for groups—if anybody came. But the project had no halls, no office, no premises of its own. The total annual income, which had to include a part-time secretary, equipment, the hiring of halls as well as my remuneration, was less than a salary of a university lecturer. I was the only worker and now I was not sure how to begin.

I decided to wander up to the shop. It is the focal point of the estate and is really several shops rolled into one, being a mini grocery supermarket, butchers, greengrocers, off-licence, newsagents, wool shop and post office. Wares were not displayed in the windows which were blocked by pegboard adorned by the mouldering remains of Christmas decorations. But the drab outside contrasted with the vitality within. The shop is an unofficial community centre where residents go to talk and mix as much as to shop. The shopkeeper later told me that initially he could not understand why people came in three times a day instead of collecting their shopping in one go. Then he realized that the shop served other needs as well as buying and selling.

Several local women are employed at the shop on a part-time basis. They chat and take an interest in customers. Sometimes the queues move at a snail-like pace as small children agonize over how to spend their pennies or as the assistant gives detailed advice on buying wool. Few people seem to mind; jokes and pretend abuse are shouted around and the chatting continues.

So I began to linger in the shop, making contacts, picking up tips about the area. In turn the shoppers began to notice me. The bevy of local mums who gathered there also orchestrated what might be termed 'initiation tests' for newcomers on the basis of which they were classified as 'stand-offish', 'too familiar' or 'alright'. My turn soon came. A woman was standing behind a pile of corned beef tins (which were not selling because of a scare about infected meat). 'Bob', she pleaded in agonized tones, 'help, quick, I've got me boobs stuck in the corned beef.' All eyes on me. To have withdrawn in dignified silence or to have rushed to remove the offending part of her anatomy would not have done. Fortunately, I retorted, 'Sorry, I don't like touching bad meat.' The laughter was the start of a bantering, joking, relationship which has continued until this day. As my wife's Glaswegian accent was also acceptable and my children were attending the local schools, I soon came to know a number of local families. A beginning had been made.

The shop soon became a centre for meeting people, gaining information and being told of people in need. However, not all residents visited the shop. Nor could it be the base for a more systematic assessment of local need. It was time to go door-knocking.

I spent much of late 1976 and early 1977 on the knocker. My procedure was to drop in a letter explaining the purpose of the project and then to call a few days later to ask people what they thought the project could and should do. I was told to clear off at one house. A dog's teeth grasped the seat of my trousers as I made a fleeing leap over the fence of another. One bubble-cut woman replied that she needed a rich bloke of about 40. I pointed out that I was not rich. Generally, though, I was welcomed, often invited in, and given a serious discussion.

That door-knocking, in the freezing weather, proved as valuable a step as I could possibly have taken. Obviously it provided contacts with a large number of people. In addition, the information which was gleaned enabled me to build up a social picture of the area.

Consider the two first streets where I visited. Of the 89 occupied houses, I had discussions with adults in 75. Of these, 10 of the 75 were one-parent families. For what it is worth, this 13 per cent of one-parent families is considerably above that for the local authority as a whole. Excluding the retired, 17 of the families did not possess a head in full-time employment, again a proportion well in excess for the whole local authority. However, it should be added that a number of these families had children at work or wives in part-time employment.

As people conversed about the area and themselves, certain worries began to emerge. Most prominent was the irregular school attendance of their own or other people's children. Next were difficulties in coping with their youngsters, especially teenagers. Criminal activities—by children and adults— were also cited. Other families complained of financial difficulties, especially if they were dependent on social security.

Three points must be made about these findings. Firstly, they were not peculiar to these two streets. In time, another eight roads were door-knocked. Secondly, the information I sought put the emphasis on problems. It should be added that many of the people I saw were cheerful copers. Indeed, I came to admire the manner in which they helped themselves and others. Thirdly, the difficulty on which most people

requested me to take immediate action concerned the noise in the street. They complained of the motorbikes, of vandalism, of youngsters shouting late at night, of kids playing knock-down-ginger, and the occasional stone through the window.

Intending to find out for myself, I began to hang about the streets at night. Kids soon observed me, some had already heard of me through their parents. At times, I felt almost threatened as they surrounded me around the lamp-post!

'Are you from the f— welfare?'

'You been talking to my mum, ain't yer?'

'Will you shop us to the police?'

'I'm on probation.'

'Are you a social worker?'

'What can you do for us girls, then?' (laughter)

'Nothing that I can't do, darling' (more laughter)

'You know Dave Wiles, don't you?'

I tried to explain why I had come to Edgetown. Told them of my interests. Got talking about the local football team. Then I said I wanted to know their views on Edgetown.

'B— awful.'

'Boring.'

'There's nothing to do.'

I began to pick up their names. Exchanged greetings in the street. I stopped to kick a ball about in the street with them. We stopped to talk again. I mentioned the complaints of some of the adults. A thick-set boy who, despite the cold weather, was wearing just a waist-coat, drainpipes and ear-rings, replied, 'Oh yer, they don't want us in the home. "Be quiet, I'm watching telly." Then they complain if we meet in the street. It makes yer sick.'

A dark-haired lad in a leather jacket momentarily relaxed his grip on a blonde slim girl, 'S'right. Where can kids have a game of football here? They complain if the ball goes in their gardens.'

Another boy, slightly cross-eyed, holes in his shoes, no pullover, paused to spit, 'Noise. You wait 'till you hear some of them mouthing it off. When old fat guts and toffee nose have a row the whole street hears about it.'

An attractive, shy girl with auburn hair spoke for the first time, 'We don't stay out here 'cos we want to. There's nowhere else to go.'

At this point I thought it timely to call a meeting at my house in order to discuss both the complaints of parents and their own grievances.

About 20 youngsters attended. They raised again the lack of cafes, the lack of somewhere to play football, of somewhere to keep dry. They pointed out that often they wished to be outside of crowded homes yet were told off if they made a noise outside or broke into the garages (the local lock-up garages which council tenants could hire) in order to keep warm. They explained how the council had recently banned motor bikes from a nearby piece of waste ground and had built on another play area. The unanimous request was for a youth club, and it was decided to elect a committee. I refused to be chairman and this position was filled by Dave Wiles, a 21-year old who had lived on the estate all his life. I explained the part the project could contribute and accepted respons-ibility—along with the committee—for organizing the club.

My first task was to find somewhere to meet. This proved harder than anticipated as the estate possessed no hall of its own. Eventually I came across some pre-fab classrooms, formerly used by the comprehensive school, but now rented by an artist. He had originally hoped to attract people to classes in the huts. The Edgetown residents had not responded and the only crowd that gathered consisted of schoolboys peering through the windows during lunch-time nude model classes. Even this came to an end and the artist was glad to make money by renting out the rooms. We agreed on a £1 an hour on Monday evenings. The Senior Club was about to start and, somewhat to my surprise, the project was about to develop with a strong emphasis on youth work.

I am very conscious that this first chapter concentrates very much on myself. Fortunately, Dave Wiles—yes, the local boy who was chairman of the club—joined the project as a full-time worker in 1977. Jane Thomas came in 1979. From now on the book can refer to 'we' and 'us'.

2 The Clubs

'This is our place'

Midnight. Another club over. We return home and five teen-agers, Dave and I unpack the van. The club gear has to be brought back after club and stored in various parts of the house. A couple begin to check the money against the cafe stock to see how much has been nicked. The kettle goes on. We record the evening's damage. One broken window, one smashed billiard cue. 'Why do we bother?' grins one lad, holding up the remains of the cue. We settle around the table clutching the mugs of coffee to warm us up and mull over the evening. Two youngsters on the run from a community school had sought refuge in the club. Their crimes were listed. 'I don't know why they do it, they must be psychos', declared Wynn, so expressing those double standards of his which never ceased to amaze us. 'You shouldn't have let them in, they don't come from Edgetown,' said Sam. Sam was one of our regulars. Honest and reliable, his comments were usually valued. He had strong feelings on club membership and didn't like letting in boys from the adjoining estate. The smoke thickened, the laughter grew until we kicked them out and Dave and I dragged ourselves to our beds.

The boys had raised two questions which must be aired in this chapter. Why do we bother with youngsters? Why do some of them get into trouble? Having discussed them, we will be in a better position to explain the emergence of our clubs and to consider whether or not they can help local kids.

WHY BOTHER?

Why should we be so concerned to stop youngsters going into public care or becoming delinquent? Pundits from what can be called the political right and political left sometimes decry efforts to help. The right may say, 'They made their bed, now let them lie in it.' 'It's their own fault if they misbehave, it'll do 'em good to be sent away.' The extreme left may argue that working-class kids get a raw deal from society and have every right to express their discontents by delinquency.

The advice of the right wing would result in many more children being sent away. Unfortunately, the removal of youngsters from their homes often does not improve them. If received into the care of a local authority they may face one foster-home breakdown after another. Of course, this is not the invariable outcome, but it does frequently happen that a child faces more instability after removal from the family. If placed in a community school — or approved school as they used to be called — they may learn more delinquency from their new friends. Thus the well-being of the child is usually better served by trying to deal with problems within the family and community.

The radical who accepts, even encourages, delinquency is not putting his own life or property at risk. Perhaps working-class youngsters are badly treated, but if they continue in delinquency, it is their freedom which is lost not that of the armchair critic. And it must be realized that boys can and do get punished for what are relatively minor crimes. The recent local crimes dealt with by the police have included stealing a ferret, money, bikes, motorbikes, trousers, gloves, plimsolls and tools; taking away, driving and damaging cars; breaking into houses, schools and halls; breaking into meters; damaging property; and snatching money from a bus driver. The total value of all these goods would not be a fraction of what one businessman may get away with by fiddling his income tax. Yet courts can and do deal with them by depriving youngsters of their liberty. As pointed out in the first chapter, once boys are sent to penal institutions there is a very high risk that they return home as confirmed criminals. Thus, for these boys' sakes, it is vital to stop them being removed at all.

Again, it it not the armchair pundit whose property is on the line. It is the residents of council estates who suffer most from vandalism, violence, break-ins, muggings and burgled meters. The well-being of both the youngsters most 'at risk' and of all families in the area lends support to the preventive aims of the project.

WHY DO THEY DO IT?

Before the project could take action, it had to ask the old questions, 'why do kids commit crimes?' 'why do they behave so badly that they have to be taken away?' 'why can some families not cope?' Three main types of explanation have been put forward. They are explanations which focus on the inadequacies of individuals, those which highlight family malfunctioning, and those which attribute blame more to the environment. Here only brief comments will be presented, but I have dealt with them in more detail in other publications.[5]

A few writers of the individualistic persuasion argue that delinquency is *transmitted genetically*. They argue not for the existence of a specific criminal gene, but rather that inherited characteristics, such as aggressiveness and impulsiveness, direct some people towards crime. My assessment is that biological factors do contribute to but cannot explain delinquency. Inherited aggression might just as well lead to an honest and successful career in sales promotion.

A more popular view is that delinquency and separation is but one of the results of *family malfunctioning*. In particular, one school highlights inadequate child rearing practices. The assumption is that the parents lack of participation in their children's play, their inconsistent discipline, their lack of a moral example, adversely affect the youngsters' characters. Their consequent behaviour makes them a problem at home, school or neighbourhood. Sometimes the parents cannot cope, sometimes the police have to intervene. In turn, when these children grow into parents they lack the capacities to deal with their offspring. The result is more generations characterized by truancy, uncontrolled tempers and family problems.

Again, although this explanation appears valid in parts, its proponents have not considered sufficiently which factors stimulate inadequate practices. Do people really learn from their parents or are their circumstances such that they are pushed into using these methods?

Reference to circumstances leads to those explanations which stress the influence of *environment*. Some writers explain that society praises wealth, consumer goods and job success, but then fails to equip lower-working-class children with the education or means to obtain them. Frustrated and alienated, they seek outlets in delinquent activities. Others say that in certain districts it is almost normal to steal and so youngsters simply conform to their environment. Again, parents are brought up in neighbourhoods where child neglect is common and so treat their children in a similar way.

Although they possess some validity, these environmental approaches can not account for all delinquency. Many children subjected to a lack of opportunities or to delinquent pressures do not themselves commit offences. Many parents are subject to adverse influences, yet still produce happy and stable families.

A further and more recent view is worth mentioning because it stresses the interaction between individuals, the family and the environment. Drs Wilson and Herbert put their finger on poverty, finding that families with low incomes were more likely to have children with behavioural problems. The parents certainly cared about their offspring but found that their poverty adversely affected them in two ways. Firstly, it made good rearing practices difficult to pursue. Patience, tolerance, participation were inhibited in noisy, overcrowded homes. Secondly, it harmed the parents' characters. Worried by debts, possible eviction and unemployment, they could become abnormally anxious or over-aggressive. The combination of child care methods and parental behaviour was seen as the explanation of the children's waywardness.[6]

So much for academic explanations. But what do the youngsters say? In a research survey, young offenders put forward two main reasons. Over one-half stated that they stole for material gain. Nearly one-fifth linked their delinquency with boredom.[7]

Edgetown troubles do not fit neatly into any of the above categories. Yet traces of each one could be applied to certain individuals. Children at risk of being separated from their parents might need help as individuals, as members of families or as part of a community. Subsequent chapters will explain how the project attempted to help them in time. But the 'boredom' issue seemed one on which immediate action could follow. Moreover, residents had complained of unruly kids while the youngsters themselves had suggested a club as a counter to boredom. Clubs were about to become a major part of the project.

THE CLUBS

Senior Club (1976–77)
For one year, the senior youth club met in the pre-fab classroom. The premises were hardly ideal. No separate toilet facilities for boys and girls. The only taps in these same loos. A shortage of electric plugs meant that the cafe had to be set up in the entrance. The classroom itself was crowded out with gear. An old table-tennis table (retrieved from a bonfire by an alert member). A snooker table without pockets. A dart board next to some board games. A record player which sometimes stirred outbreaks of dancing made difficult by an uneven, chipped floor. Each Monday 30–50 teenagers crowded in and made full use of the limited equipment.

The crowding was fortunate for the club could be bitterly cold. An ancient stove was supposed to circulate heat around the pipes. Usually it proved impossible to light. When successfully ignited, smoke belched out of the stove while water dripped from the pipes. The winter was a cold one, often icy and snowy with winds rumbling through the shaking, cracked windows. At times, wearing two thick pullovers, peering through the smoke and standing amidst the litter, we marvelled that the Edgetown youngsters still came. Perhaps, as one lad remarked, it was because, 'this is our place'.

During these early months, the youngsters were learning to cope with the club, with us and each other. Every week seemed to bring forth some incident. A running feud between two of the 17-year olds occasionally erupted into fighting and we had to intervene. Being situated on the border of Edgetown, the club also attracted some boys from a nearby area. Not only was tension created between the two groups, but the 'outsiders' had less loyalty towards the club and were suspected of pilfering from the cafe. A very disturbed older member complained weekly about everything in the club. One week he objected to the volume of the record player. When it was pointed out that everybody else wanted it loud, he retorted, 'Well, that proves how selfish they all are'. He was extremely frustrated about his inability to win a girlfriend. His 'touching up' became blatant fondling, provoking loud protests from the girls involved. A crowd of youngsters gathered round and we had to rescue him from a beating up.

Our hope was that the members themselves would deal helpfully with unexpected events. We were pleased when they handled calmly an epileptic fit experienced by one girl. Less pleasing was their reaction to a visit by the police. A disco was in progress inside the club when a police car drew up to examine the car of the young bloke acting as DJ. A stream of youngsters belted outside screaming abuse at 'the pigs'. Somewhat rattled, the policemen grabbed hold of one boy and bundled him into the panda. Despite the scene, two positive outcomes followed. Firstly, we took the chance to hold discussions with members about their reactions to the police. Secondly, we contacted the community policeman. Certain districts in the city had been given policemen on the beat. Edgetown was one and we invited him to the club. Initially, members did not know how to handle his presence. He was surrounded by a jostling mass who fired questions at him. One lad grabbed his helmet, ran into the road and attempted to direct the traffic. Fortunately, the policeman combined firmness with friendliness. He joined in a few games, made a few jokes and held some conversations. He became a friend of the project. His attitude towards offenders was that they might be warned, but eventually he would nick them. Hopefully, some youngsters perceived the more positive as well as the negative sides of police action.

During these months petty vandalism continued as the main club worry. A broken window, a bashed-in towel rack, graffiti on the wall. The committee attempted to deal with it, but found it impossible to do so during discos—when most lights were off—or when it happened in the loos. Further, the pre-fabs suffered a number of break-ins which the landlord thought must have been committed by club members. Following the cracking of a large mirror—thanks to a snooker ball thrown by a girl—he issued a stern warning. For a while, the vandalism ceased, but then broke out again. At the end of 1977 the artist/landlord complained that the brooms had not been put away and the towel rack banged in again. Although small in themselves, he felt they were the final straw. He said he admired the work we did, but wished us to do it elsewhere in more suitable premises. We appreciated his viewpoint. The club had lasted one year.

The Club at Home (1977–78)

The eviction posed the question of finding new premises. We tried pubs, schools and churches without success. Fortunately, our home was available. Its odd-shaped rooms proved convenient. What had once been a doctor's waiting room served as the club. The thick walls saved my family from going completely bonkers when the record player was on full blast. Of course, space was not available for table tennis or snooker and most time was spent talking, shouting, singing and smoking. We introduced discussions and kicked around such subjects as abortions, booze and violence. The numbers—between 20 and 30—made sustained conversation difficult. Probably the best and most hotly debated issues were capital punishment and race. In retrospect the 'club in the home' was valuable for promoting closer relationships between us all. Certainly, there was no vandalism in the home.

This period also marked an expansion of the club into other activities. A football team was formed. Some table-tennis matches were played against other teams. A visit was made to another club's disco. The occasion could hardly be called a success as the two groups did not mix and glared and shouted at each other like opposing football fans. During the summer we met for rounders and cricket. A pitch-and-put golf championship was held at the local course. The most memorable part was the play of Peter, a somewhat eccentric older member.

Disregarding all rules and conventions, he played each hole in rapid succession by ignoring all other players on the course. Moreover, he placed his ball on the tee wherever he was. Thus, even when it landed on the green, he placed it on the tee again and drove it as hard as possible. The golfing population seemed too amazed to make any protest. He charged through the course and triumphantly emerged apparently under the impression that the first one to finish was the winner.

Another venture concerned the use of video. Ray Jones, a lecturer at the local university obtained the use of the universities TV service on our behalf. Under him, club members were taught to operate the TV cameras and sound equipment. They decided to shoot a short play about shoplifting, with the youngsters playing the parts of the shop manager, policeman, magistrates, probation officer, parents and thief. The members took the play seriously with one 16-year old consulting his own probation officer as to what he should say. The whole episode—written, acted and recorded by club members—was successfully completed. It was valuable in that they began to feel and see the point of view of adults they sometimes regarded as enemies. Moreover, the sense of achievement contributed to the growing sense of oneness and togetherness. They now expected to meet together as a club.

Encouraged, the club later tried video again. Eric, a handicapped young man, wrote a script based on a clash between us and another youth club. Rehearsals were sometimes a stormy affair. Peter was revelling in his part as a disco dancer, but insisted on performing the whole time. He was particularly needling Isaac whose temper was short at the best of times. Finally, Peter, believing momentarily that he was star quality, challenged Isaac to a fight and followed up with a kick. The next moment 5′ 1″ Peter was being pursued down the street by 6′ 4″, 15-stone Isaac. The rest collapsed in laughter.

Peter was not the only one to be well cast. The members took delight in making Dave play a violent thug and me a moaning caretaker. Unfortunately, I was also sound link-man and, in the confusion of the actual recording, performed the caretaker wearing ear-phones under my cloth cap.

Even more enjoyment came from the spoof adverts which appeared between scenes. These were shot outside and consisted of a send-up of Edgetown as a holiday resort (shots of the local graffiti) and as a place to eat (shot of the hot-dog van run by a local dad). And so on. At the end, the parents came to see the finished product.

Another Hall (1978–79)
Eventually, permission was obtained to use another church hall on the border of the district. After the pre-fabs, it was luxury. A separate canteen and a warm hall. The premises were larger, although still crowded when up to 60 youngsters crammed in. Behavioural difficulties still persisted, particularly with some of the teenage girls whose damage to the toilets infuriated the caretaker. Generally, however, the now well-established relationship between us and the members made for smooth running.

Senior Club met on Mondays. By this time it was just one of a number of youth activities. Younger boys began to hang about outside the Senior Club pleading to be let in. During snowy weather we relented enough to let them into the porch. A deputation arrived at the house asking for a junior club and announcing that a committee had been formed.

Today, the project runs a senior club, a junior club (mixed), a junior club (boys), a young ones club (5–8 year olds), two boys' football teams and a girls' football team. The clubs not only meet in the halls, but go swimming, do volleyball, skating and so on.

The Club's Contribution
What contribution do the clubs make to Edgetown? Firstly, they do provide some—howbeit still inadequate—facilities for local youngsters. At the end of 1979, over 200 young people were attending the weekly activities. Secondly, the clubs could claim to reach some of the area's most needy youngsters. I have just looked through the Senior Club's membership list. Over half the boys had appeared in the courts or before educational tribunals. Thus youngsters with delinquency and school difficulties are being kept as members. At the same time, the clubs serve the whole area and so can not be dismissed or stigmatized as places for offenders. Thirdly, some members became identified with the club's attempts to promote a sense

of responsibility for others. Every now and then, the gardens of a few elderly folk were cleared, cleaned or dug over. On one occasion, over-zealous pruning resulted in one man losing his strawberry harvest. Afterwards, we confined ourselves to cutting and digging.

When members expressed interest in the problems of the handicapped—there is a sheltered workshop nearby—it was agreed to buy a washing machine for Eric. Apart from being unable to walk, Eric had restricted use of his hands and needed a specially adapted washing machine. A few older teenagers worked on Saturdays at a salvage firm and donated their earnings. Younger boys knocked on doors asking for jobs. The parents joined in enthusiastically in a sponsored boys v dads cricket and girls v mums rounders match. The £140 was raised and the local paper photographed the presentation of the machine outside the Edgetown shop. Hopefully, this part of the club's programme was giving the youngsters a more positive image of themselves.

Fourthly, the clubs could be a means for integrating some lonely, withdrawn or difficult youngsters into larger groups. The Social Services Department asked if we could help in this way with one fatherless family. The oldest girl (a schoolgirl) was already pregnant. None the less, she joined the Senior Club, made some friends, and accompanied us on a club holiday. The ten-year-old daughter came to Junior Club, but found it difficult to talk to others. She wanted to spend most of the evening close to one of the adults. This desire to monopolize provoked some tension with other children. On one occasion, having received a clout on the ear, she ran crying home. She returned with mother breathing out fire and thunder. However, after the position was explained, mum calmed down and stayed on at the club and gave some help. In time, the girl settled in and eventually made the step into Senior Club. Later, the two youngest girls from the same family also joined in. Against the family's problems, the project's contribution may seem small. But the clubs, combined with a few visits, did encourage the children to move out of the isolation of the home and make some friends.

Another example concerns Patrick. He attended a special school and was educationally backward. His younger brother already came to one of the Junior Clubs. His loving and caring parents were worried that Patrick had little life outside of home and school. We invited him to Senior Club in its earliest days. Patrick was a great darts player and we ensured that he got plenty of games. Three years later—and he is now at work —he still attends regularly.

To be fair, it must be said that not all attempts to integrate were successful. Kevin is such a case. I first met him years ago when I was asked to get two boys who refused to come down from a church roof while a service was in progress. Having persuaded Kevin and his brother to descend, I got to know them over the succeeding years. The brother subsequently settled down, but Kevin has continued to be as wild, aggressive and irresponsible as when we first met. We invited him to Senior Club several times, always with the same results. His provocative self-centred behaviour just reinforced his already unpopular image. Scraps ensued and the attempt was deemed a failure. We decided to see him on an individual basis.

A few, like Kevin, do not settle in. The majority do integrate. And another minority are just tolerated. Lionel was referred to us by the Child Guidance Clinic, with the hope that a club might be a constructive outlet for this disturbed, almost uncontrollable, nine-year old. The first evening at Junior Club he hit us like a whirlwind. Games went flying through the air as he swept through the club. A favourite ploy was to sweep all the snooker balls onto the floor. Thereafter we adopted a programme especially for Lionel. Adult leaders attempted to spend time with him, partly at quieter board games and partly at boxing or fighting on the mats. Eruptions still occured as youngsters responded in kind to his pushing and hitting and twice he ran screaming out of the club and made his way home. But, in general, the club could accept him. Lionel does not fit into the club, yet the club is the one organization, outside school, which he attends.

Fifthly, the clubs do provide a break for some parents. Most parents—and I'm one of them—are glad to have periods when their children are not around them. How much more do parents of youngsters like Lionel need a rest from constant efforts to control or protect? Lone parents particularly need some relief from the strain of coping with younger children. Daniel comes to mind. Now nearly 13, he had been associated with the project since it started. An explosive temper and the vilest language made him unpopular and even feared in the area. For a long period he was attending four of our clubs or groups as well as playing in the football team. If nothing more, the clubs were acting as a buffer between him and his family and neighbourhood for a substantial part of the week.

Sixthly, and most important, we hope that the clubs divert some youngsters away from delinquency. Some youngsters attribute their delinquency to boredom. The clubs succeeded in attracting a number of such youngsters. For a part of the week, the clubs try to offer something which is interesting yet legitimate. Of course, to attribute crime to boredom is too simple. Obviously, some bored kids do not commit offences. At the same time, it is worth pointing out that a number of the youngsters themselves say that the clubs do serve to stop them looking for trouble. In short, the clubs can be an alternative to delinquency. It is not claimed that they make a profound change to the youngsters' personalities. Instead, the clubs function to divert or deflect a few away from delinquent activities for certain periods of time. Studies suggest that once boys start going to court then they are likely to repeat that very behaviour which offends the law. Before long they can become part of a judicial system from which it is difficult to withdraw.[8] Thus, if the deflections mean that a few boys do not go to court, or go fewer times, then the clubs are making a positive contribution to prevention.

THE GROUPS

Some youngsters do not fit easily into clubs. They find them too large, too threatening. Within smaller units, which we call groups, they can receive more attention. Groups can more easily be tailored to suit the particular but similar needs of a few youngsters. Not least, it is worth noting that offences are not usually committed by large gangs. Delinquent youngsters usually act in pairs or in small groups.[9] Perhaps groups can be a means of helping them into different behaviour patterns.

As time went by, it became clear that the project was developing two kinds of groups. One was the regular planned group. The best example was known simply as Wiley, named after it's moving spirit, Dave Wiles. We had become convinced that some extra help was needed for boys from one-parent families. The organization One-Parent Families is constantly making clear the frequent poverty amongst such families. National figures reveal that fatherless children are those most vulnerable to reception into long-term public care.[10]

Of course, many lone parents do cope adequately—all credit to them. None the less, rearing a child without a partner can be a wearing and difficult task and we did notice a number of boys who seemed to lack either control of a father or the affection of a mother. But to form a group just for these youngsters would have been to invite labels like 'bastards'club'. Instead, we invited six boys from single-parent families to bring a friend and so establish Wiley. Backed by a grant from the Queen's Silver Jubilee Appeal, Wiley became a stable and popular group. It was a boys' group and, when asked, the boys decided not to extend it to girls. However, the arrival of Jane Thomas in 1979 meant the development of other groups amongst teenage girls and local mothers.

The other kind of group was the informal, irregular, almost unplanned one. A group might form just because a number of kids came round the house and started talking. Or we would often take a group of youngsters to some event as a one-off operation.

Activities
What did the groups do? Wiley soon settled into a pattern. It

met on Thursday evenings with ordinary activities such as
badminton, subutteo, football and snooker. The evening
always closed with refreshments, a quiz and a discussion. At
times, specialist tuition was arranged. A student with a background in electronics came for a term to teach the Wiley
members to make transistor radios. Canoeing instruction was
obtained. Even more exciting, the group went para-ascending
—that is being taken up into the air by a parachute drawn by
a landrover.

Short camping trips were another feature of the regular
groups. Here mention can be made of just two. In 1978, Wiley
camped at Plymouth in the grounds of the College of St John
and St Mark. We enjoyed glorious weather on a sizzling day
at Whitesand Bay. We went to the circus, played indoor football against a local team and cooked some awful meals. On
the other hand, one lad proved unruly at night and also made
an unsuccessful attempt to break into the student bar. The
principal of the college was extraordinarily welcoming and
understanding. Other officials quickly drew conclusions
about this bunch of teenagers and—wrongly—accused them of
siphoning petrol out of cars' fuel tanks.

The other camp was in the grounds of the Church of England
Children's Society children's home at Southbourne near
Bournemouth in 1979. Our cooking must have improved for
the boys consumed vast quantities. Adam, a 16-year-old,
amazed us with his appetite. After finishing the left-overs, he
spread the fat from the frying pan on to bread to make fat
sandwiches. But the most pleasing aspect was the cheerful co-
operation between our boys and the resident children. The
houseparents were pleased to have us and their attitude, no
doubt, influenced the children. Several impromptu football
and cricket matches took place while the younger residents
felt free to use our games and sports gear.

As well as camps, both the regular and irregular groups went
on a number of trips and outings. We often went together to
the cinema, to the seaside, to professional football matches, to
speedway, to the sports centre to play table tennis or to swim.

The Pay-Off
Groups can stimulate a warm feeling of being an insider. But

we believe that these groups gave rise to an even more positive pay-off.

Obviously, *discussions are easier* within a small group than in a large club. The Wiley discussions often concerned issues very close to the boys lives such as 'what's life like for mum without dad?', 'why truant?', and 'vandalism'. At other times in Wiley the boys (and adults) took it in turns to be the night's subject while the others wrote down what they liked about them, what they were good at, what job they might do and what advice they needed. The idea was to promote a more positive image of each other. Some of the best sessions were not planned at all. We often talked about delinquency and, on one occasion, the subject came up again as half-a-dozen of us shared a late cup of coffee in our kitchen after clearing away the club gear. Initially, the boys recounted their own delinquent exploits. Next they talked of why they did it. Finally, they weighed the gains and losses, the gaining of excitement and some material rewards against the heavy fines and possible loss of freedom.

Discussion is one aspect of group life. So are *new experiences*. One summer, we took six boys to London for the day. Until we went, I had never realized that these teenagers had never been to London before, never visited Regent's Park Zoo. Again, trips to ice-skating or to see other large towns less than 50 miles away could be an exciting event for our youngsters, yet taken for granted by other more affluent children. A number of boys in the locality were interested in bird-watching. We were able to extend their interest by taking them to bird and nature sancturies. If nothing else, the project was able to widen the horizons of a few youngsters.

Talk and experiences. Groups can also put the two together in what we call *'play-back'*. An example. While camping, we wandered into town with six lads who tried to enter a bingo hall. The bossy doorkeeper told them to 'clear off' and in descriptive language conveyed the message that the hall was not open to their types. The boys met aggression with aggression and a scene followed. This reaction is a common one. Somehow the tempers of swimming-bath attendants, shopowners, park-keepers etc. are often triggered off by the sight or sound of certain youngsters who then bring into play their

common responses. After the bingo incident, we returned to
camp and had the chance to 'play-back', to review what had
happened. We asked why attendants behaved in their bossy
ways, whether aggeßssion was the best response, what other
means could have been used to complain. The intimacy and
fellowship engendered by groups does facilitate self-questioning
and the possible readiness to learn together from experience.

As members saw each other frequently in the regular groups,
as discussions opened up their characters to others, as they
lived with each other at camps, so, we hoped, there would
develop a *mutual caring*. Certainly, in Wiley, they began to
notice and enquire if a member was away. Over half the
members of Wiley had truancy problems. So we were pleased
when Adam took it upon himself to get Matt to school. The
plan succeeded for two weeks then backfired. Matt was
persuading Adam to skive with him. However, when Don
began waking up Aston in the morning, the results were more
positive and more lasting. In time, we tried also to get members
to take more control over events in the club. When money
was available, we consulted them on how it should be spent.
Members began to take responsibility for organizing the games
and competitions. And when things went wrong, they were
involved in some of the decision-making. For instance, one
evening at Wiley, two of the older teenagers were constantly
at each others' throats. Eventually, I intervened as they fought,
using billiard balls and cues as weapons. Thinking—probably
wrongly—that one boy was more to blame, I kicked him out
for the evening. But he crept back in and, as we left, he stepped
behind his adversary and cracked the heavy end of the billiard
cue over his head. The boy fell, blood pouring out of a wound
which needed several stitches. Later, the matter was put to
members who suspended the culprit (and insisted that he
paid for the cue).

Not least, the groups can *facilitate closer contacts with
youngsters*. During clubs, it is difficult to spend much time
with the same youngster. Within the smaller groups, more
prolonged contact is possible. Often we have been able to
talk about the missing parent, to discuss why he has left,
what difficulties and confusions it caused, what feelings were
aroused if a new adult came into the family and whether

more contact was desirable with the parent who had gone. For a few boys, the enforced nearness brought about by camping together broke down barriers which had existed before.

Groups are not successful for all youngsters. One boy came intermittently, then tailed off. Another dropped out after being a frequent attender. But the regular group did allow us to work with a number in a more sustained and closer way than had been possible in the clubs.

OUTINGS AND HOLIDAYS

A number of small outings and short camps were arranged for the groups. At the same time, outings for larger numbers and longer holidays were also arranged. They became an acknowledged part of the project with children looking forward to the next outing and youngsters saving up for months for the holidays. It follows that they merit some mention.

Throughout the long summer holidays we often arranged outings. We had one gorgeous day at Weymouth at which I became very embarrassed when a young lady insisted that I was someone called Chalky White of the *Daily Mirror* and demanded £50 as a prize. Sometimes, outside bodies such as churches or students would organize them and we just had to go along. A fear of any organizer is that he will lose a child. We performed differently. Counting the children as they returned from Longleat we found one too many. He had clambered aboard the wrong coach.

The outings served to make a break in the summer holidays, when parents sometimes became fed-up with children being at home and when the kids became bored. They were also a means of drawing new children into the project's activities, especially those who had recently moved into the district. Yet no other justification was required than that the children enjoyed and valued them.

Longer holidays were also arranged. Every year, about 16–17 boys aged between ten and thirteen accompanied us to a camp arranged by a Christian boys movement called the Jucos. More will be said about the Jucos in later chapters.

Here it suffices to say that these are real camps. None of your wooden chalets, hot water and flush toilets. Here the boys sleep in bell-tents, wash in cold water, do press-ups in front of the flagpole and spend the day jumping in the sea, off the pier and on to tent officers. Tent officers are adults. We (Dave and Bob) had to get up at 6.30 a.m., be responsible for a tent of 7 boys, cajole or bribe them into beating all the other tents, try to prevent rain flooding their sleeping bags or hurricans blowing their tent away and keeping them quiet at night. Despite the agonies suffered by us, nearly all the boys love these camps, strike up friendships with lads from other areas, and return as often as they can.

The senior youth club holiday started by accident. A few of us had decided to take a late and cheap holiday at Butlins in 1977. Some of the members asked if they could come and eventually 20 took residence in Billy Butlin's self-catering chalets. Sharing rooms certainly brings people into close contact. Too close at times I thought, as I woke each morning with the smell of a pair of socks. Not only did the owner sleep in them, but also his trousers, shirt and all his other clothes. But then some of the boys roared with laughter because I wore pyjamas.

The first Butlins was not easy. The boys tended to be very noisy at night, while it was difficult to get the girls to keep reasonable hours. A couple of serious fights occurred between our members. Peter was proving particularly annoying. He tried to avoid any chores and drew attention to himself in the cafes by rendering loud impressions of Donald Duck. The others teased and goaded him into outbreaks of violence. Neighbouring chalets began to complain and the management warned us to quieten down or pack our bags. We moved the youngsters around in order to separate the protagonists and had a long talk with them all. One of the older boys took the initiative and apologised to the other chalets. Subsequently, the holiday progressed more smoothly until near the end when £15 was stolen from Dave Wiles' case.

Whatever our feelings about the holiday, the members considered it a success. So in 1978, an even larger party set out. A vacancy arose and we were joined by a middle-aged, unsupported mum, who had not had a holiday for years. The project had now been functioning for two years and our closer relationships with the youngsters made control much easier. Some late and boisterous nights were kept, while a couple of the girls were thrown into the fountain. But the only serious incident concerned an attempt to break into the meter in one of the chalets. We reported it to the officials and no action was taken. The cool weather meant that many hours were spent drinking coffee, playing cards and talking in the chalets and cafes. Once Peter was expounding loudly his inability to control his sexual feelings. The table included a teenage mother and a youngster with a quick temper. The group refrained from baiting Peter, for his remarks had sparked off a discussion about 'self-control'. The return journey will be remembered most for one girl's feat of covering the whole of the side of the van with sick. The little Fiat minibus was packed with bodies and luggage and Julie, feeling ill, could find no space. She opened the two side windows and her mouth. At 60 m.p.h. the devastating effect was to draw her vomit into and around the van. A nauseating experience.

In 1979, we applied too late for Butlins. The result was an even better holiday for we booked at St George's, a holiday centre at Georgeham, Devon. St George's is a large old rectory run by the Rev. David and Jackie Rudman. David and Jackie are no ordinary vicar and wife. Jackie was a former girlfriend of Mick Jagger and into the drug scene. She then experienced a conversion to Christianity and married David. With no money, they decided to buy St George's and within a few days obtained the exact amount for the deposit. Their story cannot be told here. What mattered to us was that they were a couple who not only tolerated, but actually welcomed our youngsters. We catered for ourselves, had the run of the house and, blessed with fine weather, spent the days on the beaches. By this time, Jane Thomas had joined the project and more girls accompanied us. Of course, difficulties were not unknown and we had to lay down rules about who did what at night. During one evening's walk on the front, a teenage girl decided to drown herself as she had been rejected by a boy. On running into the sea, she found that the cold water caused a change of heart. Unlike Butlins, the entertainment was not provided. In response we spent some zany hours making music, playing charades and having bonfires on the beach.

The holidays drew us together. We had to solve our mutual problems, had to share the cooking. The presence of girls meant that we (Dave and I) began to build up relationships with them. At the very least, the regular holidays mean that some youngsters, who would not otherwise do so, now get away for a week or two.[11]

CLUBS AND THE PROJECT

The clubs, the groups, the outings and the holidays became an essential part of the project. As they had a definite slot once a week, once a month, or once a year, they formed a framework for the project's workers. We had a timetable to keep. When doubting the effectiveness of the project, we could always draw comfort from the knowledge that youngsters were enjoying clubs which would not otherwise have existed. Further, the clubs initially served to give us some credibility in the neighbourhood. Social workers know how difficult it is to explain their job to lay people. How much more so for community social workers, as we tended to call ourselves. But people do know what youth clubs are and parents tend to regard them as 'a good thing'. Thus, at the start of the project, local people not only associated us with the clubs but were also pleased that activities were being organized for their children.

A chapter on clubs and groups tends not to concentrate on individuals. Yet, finally, it is necessary to make clear the hope that individuals benefit from these collective activities. Apart from 'having something to do', we believe that some youngsters gained by having a role in the clubs. Whether as cafe manager, subs collector, committee member, or football referee, they gained a status and responsibility not exercised before. At the very least, the clubs often provided a background against which conversations became more possible. For example, we found it difficult to communicate with a punk often seen in the streets. He occasionally played for our football team for which I was the veteran goal-keeper and

Dave the all-purpose defender/attacker/and taker of throw-ins. During one match, which we were winning easily, the punk and I leant against the goal-posts and began to talk for the first time. Football was the starting point.

More importantly, the interaction at the activities was a means of opening our eyes to facets not noticeable before. For instance, on holiday we saw how unpopular one lad was and so understood why he needed to capture our attention. Again, we often discovered positive sides which were not always apparent to schoolteachers or local authority social workers. This information could be vital when a boy was in court.

In 1977 Terry appeared charged with the theft of bikes, motorbikes and burglary. His school report indicated that he was a liar, thief and bully. The probation officers report could say little more. However, having seen him at the clubs and holiday, I spoke about his regularity, his footballing skills and general co-operation. Terry was fined. Two years later, now aged 17, he was convicted of taking and driving away cars without the owners' consents. The probation officer could do little more than point to his home circumstances and unemployment. Once again, I could honestly paint a more positive picture, while not decrying the serious nature of his offences. Terry had successfully participated in some adventure-type activities and always respected the youth club's property and rules. On one occasion, a can of petrol caught fire at the club's bonfire. While everyone else scattered, Terry was brave enough to throw his jacket over it to smother the flames. The magistrates welcomed this information and indicated that they had almost imposed a custodial sentence. Instead, Terry received a community service order. We never had much contact with him outside the clubs, but the individual knowledge gained there facilitated the presentation of more positive sides of Terry's behaviour.

3 The Youngsters

'Friends, helpers, policemen, relatives'

A frosty winter's morning. 8.15 a.m. I trudged up the road pulling my anorak around me. In the shop, I exchanged a few cheerful words with the mum behind the counter while buying the paper. Across the road I pushed open one gate and stepped through the long grass in the small front garden. The curtains are drawn but I don't knock. Fishing out a key, I let myself in. Upstairs I shake a boy. 'Come on, time to get up.' 'No, I've got a sore throat.' 'I'm not leaving until your feet are on the ground.' 'I hate school.' 'So do a thousand other boys.' A few shakes. A sullen face emerges, sits up, pulls on a shirt. I trudged back to say goodbye to my kids as they departed for school.

CONTACTS WITH YOUNGSTERS

The above incident was not unusual. The work of the project involved hundreds of contacts with youngsters, particularly teenagers. These contacts were in addition to those made at the clubs. The concentration on youngsters was a matter of deliberate choice. Of course, work with parents is important (and will be described in the next chapter) but early on we decided that our priority would be direct work with youngsters on the estate.

If youngsters were to be reached, if they were to feel confident enough to express their problems, then some mode of contact with them was essential. The clubs and groups were useful meeting points but were not always open when the youngsters wanted help or advice. Consequently, we allowed them to just come and knock on the door of our house. Simultaneously, we felt free to call on them.

How often was contact made and why? A diary was kept for the first three years of the project and hence it is possible to present the results shown in the tables.[12]

Table 1
Calls from youngsters to home in three-year period

No. of calls 1596
No. of persons 2577

	No.	%		No.	%
Personal relationship	644	40.3	Delinquency	45	2.8
Boredom	423	26.5	Employment	28	1.7
Club matter	179	11.2	Truancy	25	1.5
To borrow	116	7.2	To deliver message	23	1.4
Outings and holidays	75	4.6	Other	38	2.3

Over the three years, I recorded 1596 knocks on the door from youngsters (see table 1). Often more than one person came at the same time and so these calls involved 2577 youngsters. Of course, these are not different youngsters for the same ones would call again and again. The number of different youngsters with whom we worked closely in one year is given later.

The largest number of calls (40.3 per cent) concerned the *personal relationship* we had with a core of youngsters. This term will be explained later. Of all calls 423 (26.5 per cent) were from boys or girls complaining *'We're bored'*, 'I've nothing to do', 'It's freezing cold, we've nowhere to go'. Our response was usually to suggest something. During the summer, we kept swing ball in the garden for them to play. For a period we generated some enthusiasm for building go-carts. Bird-watching also went well for a while. In the colder weather, they were more likely to be invited in to play snooker or table tennis or just to listen to records. In the freezing weather, we made sledges. Sometimes the youngsters needed us to organize something. More often we just had to provide the equipment and room.

A *club activity* accounted for 179 (11.2 per cent) of the

calls. A member might be asking what time football started or whether they could change from ice skating this week to roller skating next week or 'Can my brother come to senior club, I know he's too young but I've got to look after him so I can't come unless he does?'

The 116 (7.2 per cent) calls *to borrow something* ranged from two boys wanting to borrow deposits on motorbikes (request refused!) to those wanting to use a spanner or hammer. During the summer, youngsters also borrowed the project's camping equipment. Often they camped in their back gardens but sometimes further afield.

Booking a place or paying money in for the *holidays and outings* accounted for 75 (4.6 per cent) of the calls. Boys calling to admit to or discuss the implications of a specific *delinquent activity* took up 45 (2.8 per cent) calls. For instance, a boy might call after regretting a recent break-in he had committed. More often, he had been caught and wanted to ask for help.

Talking about *employment* involved 28 (1.7 per cent) of the calls. Boys would be wanting help to find their first job after leaving school or a new job following unemployment. There were 25 (1.5 per cent) calls which saw a *truant* standing on the doorstep while 23 (1.4 per cent) had a younger child bringing a *message* from their parents. The remaining 38 calls (2.3 per cent) covered requests to repair bikes, to give lifts, to look after small children and so on.

As well as youngsters coming to us, we would go to them. Table 2 does not count organised club activities but visits to youngsters in their homes or accompanying them somewhere.

Table 2
Visits to or accompanying youngsters in three-year period

No. of visits 678					
	No.	%		No.	%
Personal relationship	284	41.8	Truancy	26	3.8
Outings and holidays	103	15.1	Employment	23	3.3
Club matter	102	15.0	Delinquency	18	2.6
To give lift	58	8.5	To go to court	16	2.3
Hospital visit	36	5.2	Other	12	1.7

The table does not give the number of youngsters involved as, when visiting a home, and a number of children emerge, it is not possible to say how many were seen.

Once again, the leading reason for a visit—284 times (41.8 per cent) involved a *personal relationship* with a particular youngster. Many calls, 205 in all (30.1 per cent) were made to sort out *holiday arrangements*—103 (15.1 per cent)—or *club matters*—102 calls (15 per cent). Lifts given to youngsters accounted for 58 (8.5 per cent) calls. We could have provided a permanent taxi service but limited lifts for such purposes as going to the doctors, to the social security office or to the Job Centre, all of which were a considerable distance away. The 36 visits (5.2 per cent) to *hospital* included both taking boys to casualty following accidents and visiting them as in-patients. On 26 occasions (3.8 per cent) *truants* were found in their homes or on the street. Smaller reasons for visits were to discuss employment, to talk about specific delinquent incidents and to accompany boys to court.

PERSONAL RELATIONSHIPS

Obviously, many of the contacts made were of a superficial nature. They were enquiries about the project's activities or requests to be given something to do. As will be shown in one year, over 70 different youngsters would call and their requests could be dealt with in a straightforward manner. But a core of about 20 youngsters needed more intensive help. Their calls and visits have been classified as 'personal relationships'. This reason constituted the largest single reason in the tables and certainly took up the bulk of our time outside club work. Much of the remainder of this chapter will be devoted to describing our personal relationships with these young people.

'Relationships' is a shorthand term which covers those whose calls or visits involved a more individual, helping relationship. Within the aims of the project, they possessed certain needs, difficulties or problems which we attempted to meet or modify. If, as is claimed, delinquency, truancy and vulnerability to being taken into care stem partially from individuals' reactions to their family, school or environment, then it seemed logical to help them cope as individuals with their responses. Thus, we made ourselves available to these young-sters at all times whether they had a specific reason for calling or not. In social work terms it might be said that we offered them casework. We preferred to call it a personal relationship. We were also content with the boy who described us as 'friends, helpers, policemen and relatives'. More flippantly we were the 'centurions'. A custom arose that, when a boy had consumed a hundred cups of tea at our home, he received his own mug—hence a centurion.

What We Stand For

So Dave Wiles and I made ourselves available to talk to, to befriend certain youngsters. Personal relationships can be used to influence people in certain directions. Thus it seemed fair to make clear to the youngsters what we stood for. In short, early on we would make clear our values and views. At the risk of over-simplification, our main values can be listed as four beliefs.

Firstly, a belief in them. Social work books talk about 'the worth of the individual' and, to be honest, such words can sound cheap in a society which allows people to be raised in poverty, in slums and in squalor. None the less, we held this belief strongly, not least because of our Christian conviction that all people are made by and valued by God. Some of the youngsters we met seemed devalued by those around them. Some were deemed failures because of their lack of progress at school. Some were written off because of their delinquency. A few were not liked even in their own homes. A number even held themselves of little worth and adopted a fatalistic 'don't care what happens to me' attitude.

Within a relationship, we wanted to show that they mattered to us. We could do this by listening to their side whatever they did, by sticking up for them and by being persons they could trust. The issue of trust came out most clearly in the question of what we would do when we knew boys had com-mitted a crime. We decided that we would not shop offenders to the police. When boys confessed delinquent exploits to us, we encouraged them to return the goods to the victims, to tell their parents or to go to the police themselves. At times, we accompanied them to the police station, but we would never inform without their consent. Thus, we hoped to show that such was the value we placed on them that we would not abuse the trust they placed in us.

Secondly, a belief in families. We believe that happiness is most likely to be found within the family unit. Of course, some children are so badly treated at home that their safety and well-being demand their removal. But, in general, our experience suggests that their personal development is best pursued through relationships with their own parents. It was envisaged that teenagers would often come to us with complaints and grumbles about their parents, would want to discuss the relationship problems they were experiencing at home. While welcoming their approaches, we did not want to become a barrier between children and parents. Consequently, we tried to make it clear that their first loyalties were to their parents. This loyalty could be expressed by the youngsters telling their parents where they were going and what they were doing. In particular, we advised them to keep parents in the picture when any trouble was brewing, for example, school action because of truancy.

Thirdly, a belief in honesty. This may seem an obvious point but it took time to establish. Some boys, while accepting our opposition to shoplifting, would urge us to fiddle our way into the Sports Centre, to take for personal use items donated to the project or to accept for the clubs goods which they could purloin from school. We felt that consistency had to be shown. The difficulty was to achieve this without creating a soft or 'holier than thou' image.

Fourthly, a belief in attending school. Truancy frequently came to our attention simply because truants knocked on the door. Some youngsters were alienated from school, others found it boring. While appreciating their dislike, we still reckoned it in the youngsters' interests to attend. If a youngster appears in court the magistrates nearly always give attention to a report from school. Our observations are that the youngster's attendance record is one of the key factors which magistrates consider in deciding his/her future. Again, evidence suggests that youngsters who stay away from school often fill in time by committing a delinquent act.[13] Not least, school

performance influences the range of options open to youngsters when leaving school. Even if winning no academic
qualifications, favourable references about reliability could
sway a prospective employer. Thus, early in the project we
expressed our opposition to playing hookey.

In practice, the living out of the beliefs was not straightforward. Our own actions did not always live up to them.
The beliefs sometimes contained contradictions. Thus we
believed in honesty but would not report a boy whom we
knew was stealing. We were inconsistent. Sometimes we
accepted a boy's account that he was too ill to go to school
and even looked after him. Later, other boys would say that
he had 'recovered' by the evening and accused us of being
soft on him but hard on them. These contradictions and
inconsistencies had to be borne. They were part of the struggle
to clarify to youngsters the aims and values of the project as
expressed in our relationships. If we made them clear then, at
least, they could have the knowledge to decide whether or
not they wished to reject what we offered.

As figures indicate, a number of youngsters did choose to
enter into personal relationships with us. Although 'personal',
the relationships varied in type and intensity. They can be
separated out as 'short-term contact', 'long-term friendship'
and 'daily relationships'. Some resulted in 'disappointments'
while in others 'some light' was seen. Examples of each of these
will now be given. Sometimes the accounts will be told in the
first person 'I', sometimes 'he' (referring to Dave Wiles) and
sometimes 'we' (when we were both involved). This may
confuse the reader but is unavoidable as sometimes I worked
with a youngster, sometimes Dave did and sometimes we did
it together.

SHORT-TERM CONTACT

A knock on the back door. John stood there.
    'Could I talk to you, Bob?'
    'Sure, come in'
I was surprised. John was one of the few lads who had openly
shown his dislike for us. He attended the clubs but criticized

them. He kept a distance from us but let us hear his snide comments.

John lived alone with his mum who worked hard in a grocer's shop. At 15, he was fed up with school and wanted to leave. Why had he now decided to approach me? I might have guessed.

'Bob, I've been nicked. Will you come to court with me? My old dear is going spare.'

John had broken into a house and raided the meter. We sat and talked about what would happen in court, about his resentment towards his absent father, about how he appreciated his mum but could not express it to her.

A month later we sat in the crowded court waiting room. A wedge-shaped corridor, it resembled the black hole of Calcutta. All cases had been told to arrive at the same time so most had a long wait. John's mum found a seat on a wooden bench while I sat on the radiator. Most were standing. Probation officers read out supposedly confidential reports while those around all listened. Witnesses and accused jostled together. Solicitors in pinstriped suits sporting silk handkerchiefs elbowed through to consult with scrubber-nut juveniles wearing bomber jackets and jeans. 'Consult' entailed the boys nodding in dazed agreement to whatever the lawyers suggested. And we waited. The court contained no refreshment facilities but I had remembered to bring some sweets. The magistrates adjourned for lunch. We went for a snack and I had the chance to talk to John's mum. She couldn't understand it. John wasn't a bad boy. If only his dad was there. John went quiet and moody. We were the first on after lunch. I spoke on John's behalf. He received a modest fine.

John was grateful. He never became as close to us as some of the other boys but he often dropped in. Skilled with his hands, he did a couple of repair jobs on the van and mended the table-tennis table. After leaving school, he had three jobs before becoming settled. He continued at the clubs. And he kept out of trouble. The period in which he needed help was short. But he appreciated it and thereafter displayed a more positive attitude towards the project.

LONG-TERM FRIENDSHIP

Some youngsters called more regularly than John without being daily visitors. For want of a better term, we describe this as long-term friendship. Three examples follow.

Colin

I met Colin two years before the project even started. Watching an informal football match, I was impressed by the speedy skills of the small, blond-haired, ten-year-old. I joined in and laughed as he slipped the ball—and himself—between my legs like a frisky wasp zooming between two broom handles. We chatted afterwards and I met his mum, for whom I developed the greatest admiration. A middle-aged divorcee, she was bringing up five children by scrubbing other people's floors and serving as a church cleaner. Living on the breadline, she was the type of person who still always had time to help others.

Once the project started, Colin became a close friend. He joined all the clubs. He played football for our teams when possible, although his time was limited by his morning and afternoon paper rounds—his contribution to the family finances. His mum was sometimes worried about the boys he mixed with, his wandering around the streets and his progress at school but, on the whole, Colin did not display the severe problems of some of the other youngsters. What role did I fill? I think I became a kind of father-figure. He lacked a man's friendship and affection and, as the years passed, we developed a cheerful, loving relationship. He rarely went away, so in 1976 he joined our family camping holiday. Subsequently, he always attended the club's holidays.

During school vacations, Colin would drop in to our home. We made a rabbit hutch together, went train-spotting and made a long trip to see his favourite football team. The years have gone by and he is now nearly sixteen. We spend time talking about his school subjects. Colin is one of the few boys in our circle taking 'O' levels, so we are reading Hemmingway together. He now calls to discuss his job applications. He is a helper at our junior clubs on Mondays and Wednesdays. On Sundays, Colin usually comes for a cuppa before accompanying our party to a local chapel.

Many of the relationships I have with boys are demanding and exhausting. Colin's company has always been refreshing. We have enjoyed common interests in football, trains and watching Worzel Gummidge on TV. Hopefully, I have given him some fatherly advice and attention which he lacked. He has given me many laughs, some spirited conversations and much encouragement.

Don

Unlike Colin, Don is no scholar. Indeed, over the three years we have known him, his dislike of school has intensified.

Don's parents are well established in the community, and he is an only child. His hard-working father and mother have always supported the project's activities. At the age of 13, Don's problems surfaced when he ran away from home for a short period. His petty thieving and vandalism resulted in an official caution from the police. We built up contact with him by encouraging his interest in bird life. With a few others, we visited a bird sanctuary and, for a while, ran a bird-interest section within one of the clubs. Don would often drop in at our home, sometimes to draw pictures of birds. He joined the Wiley Group where Dave Wiles took a special interest in him.

By the age of 14, Don's behaviour was a great trial and puzzle to his parents. He was stealing from home, a practice which continued despite some thumpings. At least twice the agitated parents called Dave to their home and asked him to get Don taken away. Dave talked with all three for hours. He pointed out how Don boasted about his dad, so that his stealing could not be seen simply as an expression of dislike between son and father. He suggested that father and son spend more time together. The stealing subsided and Don would recount his struggles to overcome nicking.

At 15, Don's main problem was attending school. He frequently came to our house at lunch time so, at least, we could ensure that he went back to his class. He now has one more year at school. By encouraging his caring parents and by seeing Don often, we hope to help him through the final year without falling into serious trouble.

Lorraine

Until Jane Thomas joined us in 1979, the bulk of the project's work was with boys. The difficulties of boys, particularly vandalism and delinquency, tended to be the ones thrust at us. Dave and I both worked more easily with boys. Further, in a small community, where comings and goings were closely observed, we felt that gossip would be provoked by teenage girls spending as much time in the house with us as did teenage lads.

None the less, some work was undertaken with girls. Lorraine was referred to us by the Social Services Department. She was a schoolgirl mother who lived with her baby, her own mother and several brothers and sisters. She had recently moved into Edgetown and her social worker felt that she was lonely and isolated. Apart from dates with the baby's father, Dennis, she rarely went out and was becoming depressed with spending so much time at home with the baby. I began calling and dutifully admired the baby. Attractive and shy, Lorraine was experiencing a stormy relationship with Dennis. Frequent, sometimes violent, arguments were followed by romantic make-ups. We dubbed it the yo-yo romance. Eventually both Lorraine and Dennis were persuaded to join the senior youth club. Lorraine began to broaden her circle of friends, accompanied the club on its Butlin's holiday and turned out for the girl's football team.

Meanwhile, Dennis was failing to provide her with any regular financial support. Lorraine applied for a maintenance order and I accompanied her to court. The crowded waiting room then became the stage for a scene. Lorraine and Dennis were the star performers, their mothers were supporting players, solicitors and myself were minor actors while other clients were the audience. The two teenagers had started with an amicable conversation which somehow became an hysterical argument. Dennis wanted to hold the baby. Lorraine refused. He retorted,

'I don't care. He's not my child anyway so I'm not paying.'
'What do you mean, he's not yours?'
'I wasn't the only one, how do I know I'm the father?'
'I like that. You're the one who's been laying it around.'
'Oh yer, what about you and . . . ?'

The audience lost interest in their own cases as the fascinating details poured out. Mothers took sides. We oldies made feeble efforts to divert them into talking about something else or to get them to eat polo mints or to change the baby's nappy. Fortunately, the usher appeared to summon us in. A magical transformation followed. As meek as a lamb, Dennis admitted paterinty and agreed to pay. Cheerfully, we all adjourned to a nearby cafe.

Exactly twelve days later my phone rang. A raging mum had discovered that Lorraine was pregnant again—by the same boy. I went round to find mum threatening to give Lorraine a good hiding and telling her to clear out. She was not so much angry with her for having sex as for getting in the family way again. Lorraine sniffed and wept that she could not always remember to take the pill. I immediately took Lorraine down to the local Maternity Unit and sat, rather self-consciously, in another crowded waiting room. We discovered that she was pregnant again. Indeed, she was so far gone that an abortion was out of the question even if she had wanted one. But Lorraine decided to keep the second baby as well. The local authority social worker made arrangements for her to enter a mother and baby home. I had long talks with mum who agreed that Lorraine could return after the birth. I also contacted Dennis, informed him of the news, and got them talking again—they had been in the midst of another row. In the following months, Lorraine continued to attend club and even managed ice skating. When her time came, she duly entered the home and produced another bouncing baby. Meanwhile, her mother, the social worker and I were making overtures to the Housing Department on the grounds that the family would now be grossly over-crowded in their small council house. The co-operative depart-ment turned up trumps, offering another house for Lorraine's mum with her children and, just down the road, a flat for Lorraine and her two. Unfortunately, the new arrangements did entail moving away from Edgetown. By this time, Dennis had hopped it and had gone to seek work in the north. Helping Lorraine to move, I felt a tinge of regret. I admired her fighting spirit. She had proved to be a co-operative club member who had served on the committee.

I had worked with Lorraine for the two years she had lived in Edgetown. The contact had been longterm but never intensive. The services offered were largely practical, sorting out finances, giving lifts, providing a few clothes for the babies. Perhaps the most important contribution was persuading her to join the youth club. If she has gained the confidence to make a wider circle of friends and interests then she may not have to seek refuge in a single relationship to the exclusion of all other considerations.

DAILY RELATIONSHIPS

Wynn

With a small number of youngsters we became involved so closely that at times not only were they calling daily but they were also spending substantial parts of the day with us. Wynn was one, a lad who gave us moments of hope and disappointment. His father worked in a garage and, although his mother was a thrifty housewife, they found it hard to make ends meet for their large family.

Wynn reminded me of the kind of boys I grew up with in London. Cheeky, quick-witted, volatile, blessed with a ready tongue, he would have made a packet as an East End barrow boy. Using these gifts, he introduced himself as soon as the project started and became a regular caller at our house. He was enthusiastic about the start of the youth club and, although only 13, soon became manager of its cafe. As I watched him quickly adding up the prices and calculating profits I wondered why he was doing so badly at maths in school

By early 1977 it became clear that Wynn had a number of problems. He tended to drift from friend to friend, appeared lonely, yet spent most of his time on the street rather than at home. He was not happy at school where he often found himself in what other boys called 'the duffers' class'. But, at this stage his main difficulty was delinquency. He arrived on the doorstep one evening to ask for help as he had to appear in court on a charge of breaking into a house. It was later revealed that he was habitually light fingered, although this was the first time he had been prosecuted. I went with him to court and his mum—not his dad—also came. He was fined. The stealing did not stop. The only crime for which he was caught involved shoplifting, but Dave and I were suspicious about items taken from our home and from the shop where Dave was employed at that time. I began to have talks with Wynn about his nicking. Some progress was made when he conceded that he did have a problem. 'I just can't stop, I want to but I can't stop,' he once declared, almost in tears. My response was to state that whatever the boredom, loneliness or despair that drove him into delinquency, our home was available to him. He took me at my word and a close friendship (punctuated by occasional outbursts) developed. He attended all the clubs, organized the refreshments at the Wiley Group and came on the holidays. He was a great member doing all he could to support the project. During the Christmas holidays, for instance, he made some Christmas cards at a local print shop in order to sell them on behalf of the Senior Club. On Christmas Day, he called five times at our home. I rarely met his father but Wynn's mother appreciated our efforts and was pleased that he was spending less time hanging around the streets. During the same holidays, his shoplifting case at last came before the court. This time I was able to speak about him to the magistrates. Wynn received a supervision order with a requirement to attend Intermediate Treatment. However, the magistrates recommended the probation officer to execute these orders by allowing Wynn to continue his close involvement with the project.

1978 saw not only a continuation of the delinquency struggle but a heightening of the battles of school. As a 14-year-old with little interest in academic work and a dislike of being told what to do, conflicts were inevitable. Relationships at home were also stormy. We continued to be available and, within this, tried to help in two directions. Firstly, by *encouraging Wynn's desire to identify with the project*. As a loner, as a boy who had few successes, as one who was not well regarded in the neighbourhood, he seemed to have little respect for himself. By giving him responsibilities within the project we hoped to build his self-confidence to the point where he could win credit and popularity for legitimate pursuits. He now became a regular helper at the Jucos junior boy's club. He responded well, howbeit he sometimes blew his top at the irritating little pests. Once, when Dave and I had to remove two youngsters who had got completely out of control, Wynn was left in charge of 20 boys for over an hour. He handled them firmly and calmly. Further, as a daily caller at our home, he became used to meeting and talking with the increasing number of outsiders who came to visit our project. He accompanied me on talks I gave about the project and had his say. He became proud of the project and proud of his part in it.

Secondly, we wanted *to discuss his emotional and social needs.* We began to talk about his home life and his friendships (or lack of them), and wondered if they were connected with his stealing. We considered how he had been brought up on the breadline and contrasted it with the easy affluence of other people. We examined the friendship between us and tried to identify what each side expected, gained and gave.

Of course, the course of events in 1978 was not smooth. Indeed, at times his behaviour reached such a pitch that we

almost despaired of any change. There were outbursts of
temper at the clubs. Sometimes he was beside himself in rage.
Occasionally, he had terrific rows at home with his brothers
and stormed out. But the main conflicts expressed themselves
at school and in stealing.

Wynn began to take more time off school. The slightest
excuse sufficed—it was snowing, it was raining and his shoes
had holes, a dental appointment had to fill a whole day as
well as his tooth.

'Sorry, Wynn', I said, as he appeared on the doorstep one
afternoon, 'I'm not going to let you in if you should be at
school.'

'It's alright, it's only games, they said I don't have to stay,'
he snarled.

I countered, 'I'll phone the school just to make sure it is
ok.'

Wynn left in a huff.

We talked much about school, about which subjects were
relevant, and which teachers he liked. I stressed the case for
obtaining a good reference even if he made little academic
progress. There were smooth periods but rows with teachers
became more frequent. Following one outburst with a senior
member of staff, he was suspended for a few days. He returned,
but shortly after had another outburst and ran out of school
in a swearing rage. He made for our house and, seeing his
condition, I let him in.

Still 1978. We sat in my car outside the house. I said wearily,
'Wynn, you know money has gone from my wallet, I believe
you've taken it.'

'That's right. Blame me. If anything goes wrong, it's always
me.'

'You know that's not true. But this time I did leave three
pounds in the wallet in my coat. You were the only one in
the room and now it's gone.'

'I tell you I f . . . well haven't got it.'

'I know you have and I want the truth. We were saying the
other day that our friendship must be built on trust and truth.'
Wynn fell silent. After a pause he grunted, 'OK, I took it. It's
alright for you. I tell you, when I went to get some dinner at
home there was nothing there. My brothers had taken the lot.

If you're hungry you just feed yourself, there's always something there.'

I retrieved the money—that time. But within a month his mum knocked on the door. A powerful woman, her moods towards Wynn alternated between protective love and raging anger. 'He's done it this time, he's nicked my purse and scarpered,' she explained. Wynn eventually returned having slept rough for a night. As usual, initially he denied the theft with great vehemence but subsequently admitted he had taken it with another boy.

A lull followed until one day he arrived and indignantly declared that he was suspected of another theft. A report in the local paper stated that the police were looking for a boy with certain tattoo marks suspected of stealing from the swimming bath's changing rooms. He exclaimed, 'Yes, I was there. I've got tattoos. But it wasn't me. You know I'm broke. They're sure to pin it on me.'

Dave Wiles was with us and suggested that Wynn take the initiative and go to the police. Dave accompanied him and, after some questioning, the police agreed that the evidence was not conclusive. At the time we considered something had been achieved by showing Wynn that he was not always without a fair hearing. Sadly, the grapevine of local lads later informed us that Wynn had conned us.

A few days later, our local policeman arrived with Wynn by his side. For a moment I thought the policeman, Eamonn, was just dropping in for a drink.

'Evening Wynn. Hi Eamonn. What do you want, a cup of tea or a quiet drag where the inspector can't see you?'

'I'll have both', retorted Eammon, 'but I've also got to deal with this young friend of yours. He's been on that old piece of junk he calls a moped again. I've warned him before it's dangerous, he's dangerous. I'm nicking him this time.'

Eamonn penned a list of charges as long as his arm. Wynn sat silent and grumpy. He refused to tell his parents and asked if I'd tell his mum. I tried to talk with him about his lack of communication with his dad but did not get very far. Later he was fined for the moped offences.

Before 1978 was out, the school phoned to report that Wynn had been stealing dinner tickets. On investigation, I found that he had been receiving them from another boy who had committed the theft. The boys then sold the ticket at less than the school price. The school were insisting on prosecuting the thief and so Wynn was drawn in. Soon after, in company with Kent (see p. 75), he stole £15 from club funds. However, Dave and I discovered the theft quickly and retrieved the money.

Thus, during 1978 Wynn's school and delinquency problems were at a height. We responded by allowing him to be with us as much as possible. He came to the house nearly every day, sometimes to play records, sometimes to watch TV. He stayed to meals and almost became part of the family. And along with the setbacks and disappointments, he developed many positive aspects. He exercised more responsibility within the clubs by doing the cafe accounts. I entrusted him with money to buy food and records. He was extremely helpful at the camps, putting up the tents, doing the cooking, clearing up. He refused to join the lad who attempted to break into a bar while at camp. At other times, he chose to stay by us in order to avoid the company of those who were planning delinquent activities. In addition, I had introduced Wynn to a friend of mine who was a trampoline coach. They spent some happy times together and Wynn won some official certificates for his proficiency on the trampoline.

One factor proved enlightening. For a couple of months, Wynn obtained an evening job at a restaurant. The money in his pocket, his interest in cooking, and a way of filling his time, seemed to settle him for a while. It suggested that he would do better in employment than at school. So 1978 drew to a close. Oddly enough, it was a year in which Wynn did not appear in court on any theft charge.

At the start of 1979, Dave Wiles and I again reviewed the position. We agreed that our objectives would be *to encourage Wynn to complete his schooling*, to continue to offer our company as an alternative to finding trouble, and to keep talking with him about his difficulties.

Wynn had two terms left at school. For some of the less academic boys, the school was developing a work experience scheme in which they spent two or three days a week with a local firm. A teacher requested that Wynn (and another lad) be attached to the project. We agreed on condition that they undertook to attend school regularly on the other days. The agreement was taken seriously with each participant signing a document.

Wynn welcomed the new status and responsibility. We taught him how to bank the clubs' monies. He set up the clubs and began to organize the games. He undertook much of the door-knocking to raise the football teams. One evening, when a younger boy was contemplating theft, Wynn persuaded him against it and instead took him out for some chips. He even baby-sat for a lone mum so that she could go out.

The work experience agreement did ensure that Wynn attended school regularly. But progress while at school was not all smooth. Following a couple of outbursts, he was ordered out and banned from a catering course which he enjoyed. A senior teacher brought him to our house. We talked about the incident for much of the day, about his reactions to orders, about his desire to do the catering course. Finally, he decided to write a letter of apology. With my help—for he is a poor speller—he composed the letter and was eventually accepted back on the course. At the same time, a more positive development saw Wynn writing about the project as part of his CSE in English. He also spoke about it at his oral where, according to inside information, he was never short of words.

Wynn was seeing us every day. At times, Dave and I worried whether he was becoming too dependent upon us for we did not want to hinder his relationship with his parents. However, the fact was that he would not spend time at home. The choice was between wandering at large or being with us. We hoped the latter was *an alternative to trouble*. Certainly his mother saw it as such and often expressed her gratitude for the attention and time we gave to her son.

The frequency with which we saw Wynn can be seen in the following account of one week in January 1979.

Monday: Morning, Wynn and John called in for coffee. As usual on Mondays, they were out shopping for the school's cookery course and popped in to see us.
Afternoon, a teacher brought Wynn round as he had been fighting and had got out of control.

Evening, Wynn was lonely and came round for the evening.

	Evening, Wynn was lonely and came round for the evening.
Tuesday:	Wynn came for the whole day as part of the work experience course.
Wednesday:	Evening, Wynn came to see us.
Thurday:	Work experience day. In afternoon, on his own initiative, Wynn visited the school to suggest that other boys write about the project in their English lesson! Evening, Wynn helped at the Wiley Group and then returned home.
Friday:	Evening, Wynn came in for a chat.
Saturday:	Morning, Wynn called in for coffee. Afternoon, with other boys, Wynn accompanied us to a football match.
Sunday:	Morning, Wynn came round and washed the minibus. Evening, 10 p.m., Wynn knocked with his face bleeding and a tooth forced sideways and in front of his other teeth. Following a row over which TV programme to have on, his brother had inflicted the damage. Patched him up and dosed him with panadol.

Clearly the relationship with Wynn was a close one. His affection was shown in the goodies, cooked at the catering course, which he presented to us, and in the hugs he gave to my wife. Within the closeness, we wanted *to talk to him* about why he needed to come and what progress was being made. He spoke about his unhappiness along with his unwillingness to stay at home. We suggested ways of improving communication, of doing things together with his family—to little effect. Simultaneously, we tried to chart his nicking to see if it was decreasing, to assess whether it occurred just when he was short of money or when he had experienced some upset.

Meanwhile, in February 1979, he appeared in court on the dinner ticket charge. For receiving two tickets valued at 40p he was fined £40. £25 was still outstanding from his moped offences. As parental income was under £50 a week, it was difficult to make payment. Soon after, he was summoned back to court and warned about the consequences of not clearing his arrears. We now worked together on a schedule to make regular payments. But our friendship was about to be shattered.

One Saturday we took a bevy of boys to the Railway Museum in Swindon. On returning, Dave and I dashed to the local hospital where my son was quite seriously ill with osteomyelitis. We came home at tea time. Dave, white faced, came down from his room, 'Bob, the holiday money's been stolen.' Dave held out the empty cash box which he had stored in his bedroom. £60, the club members' deposits, was missing. After admitting we were idiots to leave so much in the house, we voiced our suspicions. Outside of ourselves, only Wynn knew where it was kept. Moreover, one of our front door keys had disappeared within the last week. It could have been lost as a result of the slipshod, rushing life of our household or it could have been stolen.

We went to Wynn's mother. Father was out. Her lips tightened, 'I'll get the truth out of him, even if I have to beat it out.'

Her oldest son, equipped with the build of Joe Bugner, offered the use of his fists but was told, in no uncertain terms, to shut his face. By this time, the news had spread through the streets. Parents indicated what they would do if given half the chance. An angry boy told us that Wynn did have the key.

Feeling sick with anger and disappointment, Dave and I went home for a drink. At no stage in the project did I feel more overwhelmed. I was worried about my son. He was on a drip and my wife and I were taking it in turns to be with him the whole time. The thief had probably known of our absence at the hospital and taken advantage. The door kept being knocked:

'Is it true, then?'

'Yes, the money has gone.'

'Did Wynn really take it?'

'I don't know.'

'You shouldn't have trusted him. He's always been a thief. He'll never change, you know.'

'Perhaps not.'

'What will happen about the holiday?'

'You'll still go.'

In the evening we were summoned to Wynn's house. Despite my sense of personal grievance, my sympathies began to extend towards Wynn. The scene reminded me of a prisoner under the interrogation of the Gestapo. The orange-yellow rays of the street lamps flickered through the window and cast a hue over the sweating Wynn. He was sunk deep in an armchair. His father was absent. The man from next door was there as some suspicion had been cast on his son. Wynn's large brother stood behind the settee, glowering out his hostility. Wynn vehemently and consistently stated his innocence. But he admitted he had the key and returned it. His mother now produced a horse whip.

'I want the truth. Have you had that money?'

'No.' The whip came down on his thighs.

'Have you got it?'

'No, I keep telling you.' The weapon descended again and again, across his buttocks, thighs ánd arms.

The brother leaned across, 'Bob, give me five minutes with him, I'll get the truth.'

I shook my head. Dave and I put a stop to the beating and I took Wynn outside. My hand on his shoulder, I looked him in the eyes, 'Wynn, we've been through a lot together. Don't make this the end of the road. You've stolen from us before. You had the key. I believe you've taken the money. Tell me the truth. It will be tough afterwards, the boys will be against you, the parents already want your blood. But we won't shop you.' He looked up at me, shook his head and walked away.

Half an hour later, Wynn and another boy came to the house. They placed £50 on the kitchen table. They had each spent £5. The other lad said that Wynn had been boasting about having the key and he had persuaded Wynn to do the job. They both agreed to repay the £5 and I walked sadly up to tell Wynn's mum.

It was never the same again. The youngsters were enraged, and one boy put fear into Wynn by continually challenging him to a scrap. One father was prominent in criticizing me for not taking Wynn to the police. (Oddly enough, his own son was later involved in nicking and he changed his mind.) Wynn dropped out of the holiday. Club members would not let him handle money again and he had to stop running the cafes.

What happened afterwards? Within a few days he repaid

the £5. We felt that some punishment had to be imposed and, with his mother's agreement, decided that he could not come inside our house for three months. He wanted to make amends, although he could not talk about the incident. He visited my son in hospital. He occasionally turned up at church. He would call and ask us to pay in the money for his fine until that was completed. He got his CSE in English, left school and immediately found a job. It involved starting early in the morning, finishing at noon and contained opportunities for a number of perks. He stuck at the job and soon had the money to put down for his own motorbike. Further, he started going steady with a girl. He still called in, he helped dig the garden, he always conversed in the street. But he did not need us as in the ways of old.

Writing six months after the completion of the first three years, a postscript can now be added. Wynn's motorbike was stolen. He sought out the thief and was enraged when the police decided there was not enough evidence to prosecute. He calls more. Recently, for the first time, he raised the subject of his theft. He tried to explain how devastated he had felt to lose our trust. Most important, to date he has not committed any more offences.

Aston

A thick-set 18-year-old, clad in a leather jacket stood at the door. Combing his black hair, he drawled, 'Aw, Bob, there's a new kid keeps crying in the street. I've told him to come to you but he won't. Can you do something about it? Bye.'

'Thanks, I'll come up', I yelled after him. I smiled to myself. The 18-year-old was a tough lad, liked to think he could hold his drink, always ready for a fight, critical of anyone in authority. Yet here he was showing a softer side to his character.

The young kid was 11-year-old Aston. Despite the tears, he was a toughie himself. Perhaps the hardships of his life had made him so. His parents' marriage had been stormy and eventually they had split up. He had shuffled between them but had now been re-housed with his mum in Edgetown. He squatted on the kerb, head in his arms. I sat down beside him, 'Hi, Aston, I'm Bob. Have the others told about our project?'

He nodded without looking up. I went on talking, telling him about the clubs. He breathed out hostility and suspicion. I asked if he'd like to talk over a cup of tea in my house. He refused.

As the day progressed, I nodded to him several times in the street. Late in the afternoon, some younger boys knocked. Aston, looking embarrassed, was hovering in the background.

'Bob, Aston would like to see you.'

'Thanks, lads, have a game of swingball in the garden. I'll have a cuppa with Aston.'

Aston was still silent. We drank the tea. Suddenly the tears began to flow. 'It's my mum. She says she's going to do herself in. She didn't want to come here. She thinks it's a dump. She's fed up. She wants my brothers back.'

We talked. About the pain experienced by his parents; about the load he was having to carry; about the kind of life he could expect in Edgetown. Suddenly, he halted as though regretting that he had said so much. He left.

I called on Aston's mum. She was bitter about the family break-up. She felt that being housed in Edgetown was a let-down and she hadn't taken to the neighbours. Yes, she could have done herself in but she was alright now. Although disliking housework, she emphasized that she always earned her own living and refused to draw social security. She left early in the morning for her job and was proud of her record at the same firm.

After the initial meeting with Aston, it took time to build up contact again. He seemed uncomfortable in my presence and kept his distance. I observed that he was a strong lad who looked older than his years. He seemed touchy and was ready to use his fists when provoked. Then, to my surprise, he called round and asked me to help mend his bike. He called again. By this time it was the summer holidays and he asked if I would take him and a few others swimming. He joined in the summer play scheme, although he was never at ease in large numbers. We began to appreciate each other's company. He enjoyed wrestling with me. I noticed that he never used his strength for bullying others. Indeed, he tended to protect smaller boys. But the mutual appreciation was not the reason why I wanted to get closer to Aston. Two trends were causing

some worry. Firstly, I saw that he was on the fringe of delinquency. Tool kits, keys, bike spares were a temptation to him.
Secondly, returning home one afternoon (I had been in court
all day), I found Aston sitting outside the back door waiting
for me. He had taken a day off school. On investigation, I
found that truancy was beginning to be a problem. I went to
see mum again. She admitted that, as she left so early in the
morning, she could never be sure what Aston got up to. She
was never friendly towards me—and certainly very critical
behind my back—but she welcomed my efforts to occupy
Aston and even gave me a key to the house.

It was now the beginning of 1978 and I had known Aston
for a few months. Dave Wiles had joined the project and we
agreed that during 1978 we should try generally to fill some
of the emotional gaps caused by his restricted home life and
more specifically to ensure that he attended school.

A cold winter's evening in early 1978. Aston stood shivering
on the doorstep. Alone in his house, the meter had run out
and he had no cash for light, heat or food. He was a little
reluctant to come in saying that my wife—of whom he was
fond—and I needed time together. Of course, we persuaded
him in. We offered him food to supplement his daily diet of a
bag of chips but he would not take more than tea and biscuits.
We watched TV together. And so it continued. He came when
his house was burgalled and he did not know what to do. He
came when he was all alone in the house. He came when he
was bored.

At this stage, Aston was attending junior clubs on Monday
and Tuesday along with the Wiley Group on Thursday. On
Saturdays he usually played in one of the football teams. In
between, often in the company of Wynn, he called for company
to do some drawing, to discuss the clubs. He was keen to do
his part, to clear up, to wash the van, not to stay too late. It
was his idea to raise money for the handicapped person and
he led the way by earning money by washing up in a hotel—
his size was such that he passed for a sixteen-year-old.

Several times, he inadvertantly called me 'dad'. My wife
and I could not be his parents but we did want to give him
some of the experiences of a warm, family life. On his birthday, my wife, Annette, made him a cake and, with Dave Wiles

and my children, we went on a ramble together. Sadly, the cards we gave him were the only ones he received. When he had hospital appointments, we were glad to take him as his mum did not wish to take time off work. And when he had to enter hospital for a minor operation, we took him in and brought him home. On the return trip, I recall saying cheerfully how good it would be for him to get home again. When we arrived at his house, it was a Sunday, there was no one in. My wife would not leave him alone so he came back with us.

At times, it was easy to see why Aston lapsed into silent moodiness. I could understand why he preferred to stay in the rainy streets rather than go home. Almost invariably, he began to play with fire. He stole a tool box from a car. Once, out of bravado, he nicked goods from a police car while the policemen were questioning someone inside a local house. Some of his aggression was vented in outbursts of vandalism. He received a police caution. In December, still aged 12, some local boys brought him in drunk.

The vandalism and minor delinquency troubled us less than his increasing truancy. In the middle of the year, he began calling in during school time—saying he was too ill to go to school. I would take him to the doctors who would agree that his tonsils were inflamed (he subsequently had an operation) and that he could stay off school. However, having spent the day with me, he would then recover sufficiently to play football in the street in the evening. We often had words as I argued that if he could stay out late then he was well enough for school.

The truancy continued even when not ill. Warnings from the school and his mum sufficed for a few days. Then it started again. He appeared on my doorstep with another, older truant. Aston just said that he did not like school and wasn't going to go. I went over the implications of staying away. I offered to accompany them back to school. They declined. I refused to let them in. A short time later, Aston returned on his own and asked me to take him back.

I visited the schoolteachers and, with his mother's permission, it was planned that the school would phone me in the mornings if Aston had not turned up. With no one to raise him in the mornings, he was often just sleeping in. Thus, towards the end of 1978, I would often appear at about 9.30 a.m. to shake Aston out of bed and direct him to school.

By the beginning of 1979 Aston, now aged 13, had formed a close friendship with us. Yet his apathy and aimlessness was a worrying feature. Although he had moved up to Senior Club, he often preferred to walk into town to play the machines or just stand around smoking. The local policeman chatted with me about his concern that a boy of Aston's age should be out on the streets late at night. Aston just shrugged his shoulders when the matter was raised. One morning I entered his house and found him fully clothed, fast asleep on the settee. He had just dropped there when arriving home late the previous night. Then, during the spring, the truancy intensified. A teacher would phone me if Aston failed to turn up but I would still have great difficulty in getting him out of bed. The school convened a meeting of teachers, his mum and myself. His mother—annoyed at having to miss work—said that 'yes' he had to go to school and 'no' he could not drop the subjects he found difficult (a reason Aston was giving for missing school). The teachers were worried about his truancy, his 'couldn't care less' attitude, his refusal to wear school uniform, his losing of books and his failure to attain anywhere near his ability level. Some teachers wanted to suspend him from school. I managed to resist this move on the grounds that it would prove counter-productive.

Aston and I had a long talk following this meeting. He realized the implications. He knew of other boys whose school problems had finally resulted in a care order and removal from home. He had talked to one boy and did not like the sound of going to a children's home or community school. At the same time, he vehemently protested that he hated school, was bored by it, could not stand being told what to do and sometimes felt that he would explode.

Dave and I now decided to concentrate on *promoting some self-motivation and confidence* in Aston. At times, he appeared amost overwhelmed by his own apathy, lack of purpose and acceptance of failure. Given his background and circumstances, these feelings were understandable but only served to reinforce his problems. He needed to believe in himself, to value himself more highly.

One opportunity did open up. Aston was not good or keen enough to play for the school football team. But we now moved him into our Senior Club team. Even at 13 his build was such that he could challenge 18-year-olds. He was praised for his efforts and established a regular place. The football fixtures became a highlight for him. Wearing the club shirt, borrowed shorts and socks, and my plimsolls, he developed into an effective left back. He enjoyed 'cropping' and having a few words with opposing players, but also displayed much skill.

Simultaneously, he began to help at Junior Club. He put up the heavy gear as well as collecting the subs and serving in the cafe. Gradually he was mixing more. Even so, it was with great difficulty that I persuaded him to accompany the Wiley Group to its camp at Bournemouth. Once there, he enjoyed it. To our surprise, for he was not a regular at Senior Club, he decided to join the club holiday at St George's. Perhaps the telling factor was that this holiday was in schooltime. He began to participate more and during charades was prancing around in a bikini. His popularity at the holidays did something to boost his spirits.

Attempts were also made to encourage his academic performances. Dave Wiles' girlfriend, Donna, lent a hand with maths while Annette could teach French. These were spasmodic efforts and we somtimes felt defeated when he showed us his exercise books with pages torn out by his mum to use for notes. None the less, he obtained some good marks which confirmed our impression that he could do well at school. He was off-hand in his reactions, but he showed us the marks and was obviously pleased.

Another aspect of building up his sense of worth, was to continue to show our affection for him. When he was ill again he would spend the whole day at our house. He often came to watch TV or drink tea. On his birthday we clubbed together and bought him some football boots. He always found it hard to say thanks but he was over the moon. Affection, or any form of softness, were feelings he could rarely express. So I was moved, after my aunt died, when he sought me out to mumble his condolences. More positively, he would sometimes put his hand on our shoulders to express his friendship. Small signs but important ones from a boy who had always kept others at a distance.

In addition to developing his motivation and confidence, we wanted to *show him that affection and control could go together*. At home, in the street, at school, Aston had met aggression and attempts to control him. He saw this as evidence that he was disliked and his response was to defy the control either by his aggression or by sullen withdrawal. As he once stated to me in the early days, 'I've no one who can control me and I don't want affection.'

The truancy issue was one in which I could try to control and care. Here is an incident.

9.30 a.m. The school phoned to report his absence. I found him in bed and gave him a shake.

'C'mon, Aston, the school's phoned up.'

'I don't want to go. I've over-slept,' he groaned.

'That's obvious, but you are still going,' I grinned.

'I don't want to. It's too late now. I'll go this afternoon.' His voice was expressing his anger.

'Look, Aston, I know you dislike school. But what's the alternative?'

'I know, I know, same as what happened to Bert.' Bert was a teenager recently subjected to a care order.

'Could be. Some teachers want action. Isn't it better to endure school until you are sixteen rather than go through what he is?'

The conversation continued along these themes until his face emerged from the blankets. Scowling, he swung his legs over the side. He pulled a shirt on. He had no pyjamas to take off and never wore a vest. I went downstairs to see about breakfast. The larder contained some coffee and a bag of sugar. Nothing else. I put the kettle on and nipped over to the shop to buy some biscuits. We munched breakfast in silence. He was infuriatingly slow. We drove to school and I insisted on taking him in—he'd been known to disappear between leaving my car and entering the school gates. Streams of youngsters greeted us.

'Hi, Bob.'

'What you doing here, then?'

'Skiving again, Aston? Naughty boy.'

I knocked at the classroom door and went to leave. Aston called out, 'See you tonight, Bob.'

After one bad patch when the school were phoning me every day and when he was running off after being taken to school, I resorted to telling his mother. I was reluctant to do so because it meant aggro for him. On the other hand, I felt she had a right to know. I knocked to see her in the evening. Aston, knowing I was coming, shot out of the back door. His mum ranted and raved about him. She pointed out that she was working hard and he was contributing nothing. Somehow we got on to bringing back the birch, the cat and hanging. Focusing on Aston, I said that getting up in time for school was a major problem. True, mum woke him at 6.45 a.m. but when she left he invariably went back to sleep. Even an alarm clock did not rouse him. She agreed that, in future, I would sometimes wake him at about 8.15 a.m. Later that night, Aston called to see me. I recall his words, 'I'm fed up with her. I don't want to go to my dad. I don't want to go into care.'

We talked over the possibility of going into care. Aston's exploits, his truancies and his late nights had brought him to the attention of the Social Services Department. I explained that it did not necessarily mean going into an institution but could mean a foster home. He replied, 'I might not like that. Besides, I've got friends here now. Best to stay.'

Thereafter, I began to wake Aston up in the morning or, at least, ensure that he was up. Sometimes I drove him to school but usually not, for I did not want to be a taxi service. Simultaneously, he began to come to my house at lunch times. Those old inhibitions about not eating much had passed away. The system worked. He was sometimes late. Occasionally he truanted and I would find him hiding in a shed or in the public toilets. Generally, however, the summer of 1979 proved a stable period during which he was mostly at school.

By insisting that Aston went to school, I hoped that he could perceive that control and affection could go together. As a father, I like to know what my children do at night and set times by which they must come home. My wife told me that Aston, after seeing me dealing with my son, turned to her and commented, 'David has a good dad. He keeps him under control.' If Aston really grasps this point then perhaps he will not have to regard his parent, teachers, the police and other authority figures as enemies because they have to impose discipline.

We have known Aston for over two years. His delinquent tendencies seem modified. His aggression is more under control. These particular advances may not be due to our involvement, they may be due to other influences or just reflect his growing up. None the less, his teachers believe that without the project's involvement his truancy would have escalated into a major crisis requiring statutory intervention. This may yet happen but, at least, it will have been postponed. The most significant failure has been my inability to work positively with mum.

Recently, I returned home at 10.45 p.m. one evening to find Aston sitting hunched up on the kerb. I invited him in where his face red with anger, he explained that his mum would not let him go to the doctors the next day (his eye was discharging) and said he must go to school. He had stormed out. I pointed out that her desire for him to attend showed her concern about his education. I emphasized again how his mum did work to support the home. He agreed but made it clear that he wanted other expressions of parental concern like warmth, praise and company. Hopefully, this will come in the future.

DISAPPOINTMENTS

The project's involvement with Aston is still at its height. With two other boys it is at a low ebb and we cannot claim to have made much impact on them.

Daniel

Many of the youngsters with whom we work come from low-income families. Our experiences tend to confirm the findings of Wilson and Herbert (as outlined in chapter 2) that families facing perpetual worries about money, accommodation and jobs find it much more difficult to bring up their children. The result can be that their children face personal problems which otherwise might have been avoided. However, with other families the difficulties seem unrelated to these factors.

Daniel is such a case. His hardworking parents had provided a well-furnished home, they expressed love for him and always defended him to the full. But he was frequently left to his own devices, was allowed out on the streets until late at night and had very little control exercised over him. His jutting, belligerent face, his foul language and readiness to resort to violence soon earned him a bad reputation. Yet, he also possessed charming, articulate and intelligent features which enabled him to escape from many tricky situations.

We met when Daniel was ten. He joined the clubs with enthusiasm. He accompanied us to the Jucos' (boys' club) camp of the summer where his problems forcibly presented themselves. The running of the camps required boys to accept certain duties—to clean up their sleeping-kit in the morning, to keep the tent clean, to take a turn in washing-up. These duties became the more necessary as the rain was tumbling down much of the time, so that clothes and gear were getting drenched. Daniel just refused. If other boys remonstrated with his lack of participation he would hurl himself at them kicking and punching. If adults intervened he might well tear away and disappear for an hour. When asked to wash-up he replied, 'Why should I do it just to help others?' Fortunately, these periods were interspersed with others when he would suddenly seem co-operative and amenable.

As the week progressed I found myself frequently beside him. At times I had to hold him down forcibly until he was settled. One evening I sat alone with him in his tent. I had joined him there as he refused to mix with the other 70 boys in the large marquee. The rain was beating like a drum on the canvas, the guy ropes were creaking and straining. I wondered if he was homesick and wanted to go back early

'Of course not, I like camping.'

'That's good. But a lot's gone wrong today.'

'That's not my fault. They've been picking on me.'

'No, its not just their fault. I know its not all you, but I have watched you flare up when asked to do the same as the others.'

'No, I haven't. Nobody tells me what to do. This is supposed to be a holiday not a prison.'

And so we went round in circles. At the end I said, 'Daniel,

I don't know what's biting you. Something is. But if you want some friendships in the coming years, then you can come to Dave and me.' His face continued to show defiance, bitterness and sadness.

At the end of the camp I took a few boys and the gear in the minibus. Dave accompanied the rest of our party on the train. Here Daniel gradually became more and more out of hand. Finally, they reached the home station where my wife waited with the car. Dave had just remonstrated with Daniel for playing about with trucks on the platform. In response, Daniel decided to run away. Dave caught him and held him down and managed to get him in the car with Daniel struggling and swearing. They delivered him to his door. where his mother expressed little surprise, but said the holiday must have got on top of him.

The camp was followed by the project's play scheme. Daniel now rejected us, was destructive, declared the scheme to be lousy, yet still came every day. On the final day, his running hostility with an older boy ended with a fight in the street with the latter receiving the two largest black eyes I have ever seen.

These events contained a cycle of behaviour which was to be repeated every three to four months for three years. These are the stages.

1 A period of enthusiasm. At this point, Daniel is a keen club member, attends regularly and is helpful. He even admires our work and once commented, 'I want to do your job when I leave school. How many 'O' levels do you need?' The leaders begin to think to themselves, 'This boy has been mis-judged.'

2 The attempt at self-control. Thus on the football field he puts through his own goal and does no more than let out a few curses. When I took him to a tattoo (the military kind) at Cardiff, he managed well until we had a long wait at the station on the way back. Then he began to irritate passengers with his antics on the platform.

3 The niggling phase. Here Daniel seems to want to undermine others. His hostility is aimed at particular individuals rather than everyone. On my birthday, I received a card

from him on which he had written a nice message to me then 'Down with parents'. At the time he was complaining that his parents wouldn't let him do anything, that is, they would not give him more money. At other times, he campaigned against certain adults by throwing stones at their houses and calling them names. More usually, the target is another boy whom he constantly nudges, trips up or whose bike he damages.

At a visit to London Zoo, he took delight in niggling and cheeking a zoo keeper until an outburst followed. Apparently, he was shoplifting from the large toy shop we visited on that same day. While visiting Don in hospital, Daniel made a pest of himself. He tore up and down the corridors on an invalid chair and swore at nurses who reprimanded him. Eventually, the matron blamed Don's parents for allowing Daniel to come. Still the incidents occurred until the hospital authorities made Don leave.

4 The eruption. The niggling finally builds up into an explosion. At this stage, he seems to reach a pitch in which he becomes physically wild and has to be controlled. Two examples will illustrate this period.

We were at a large-scale rally in which our boys were competing against others in a number of team events. He was in a trouble-making mood. I had to retrieve some stolen goods from him. He was disrupting the team events, picking fights, swearing at adults and tearing around the buildings. Pressure was put upon us by officials to control him. Everytime Dave or I approached him, he ran away. Eventually, he tried to persuade another boy to run off and hitch-hike back home. I felt I had to intervene. We were in an urban area, miles from home, and it was getting dark. Anthing could have happened to two boys on the road. I told them to come back. One boy obeyed. Daniel started to run down the street with me in hot pursuit. After thirty yards, I caught him as he struggled and kicked. At this point, a motor bike stopped and a tough young man in a leather jacket got off; 'What are you doing with that kid? Leave him alone.'

My patience was at an end and my reply was not polite. He rejoined, 'If you want to fight, do it with me.'

I was having enough trouble holding down Daniel, let alone taking on the well-meaning rocker. Fortunately, Dave Wiles arrived and explained what was happening. We then had to drive home with Dave stopping Daniel from jumping out. At his home, we explained what had happened. His parents couldn't imagine 'what had got into him' and made no protest when he ran out of the door.

Another time, at one of our small groups, he was again on the boil. The boys were making radios when Daniel, annoyed at his lack of progress, grabbed a soldering iron and lunged at the face of another boy. The latter parried the blow and clouted him round the ear. That blow lit the fuse. Daniel attacked another, older boy with a badminton racket and we had to intervene to stop his retaliation. He then kept running in to ruin a game by pinching the snooker balls off the table. We tried to speak to him, to comfort him. He abruptly turned away, declaring he would smash some windows. He had to be stopped and again Dave and I had to struggle to take him home. Even there he was beside himself with rage. His mother told him to sit down and I let him go. Incredibly, he leapt across the room, undid the window and was almost out. Fearful that he would do serious damage to himself or others, I grabbed his coat. His face contorted with rage, he grabbed a garden fork which was outside the window and turned back on me. I swung him around while Dave, who had dashed outside, disarmed him. For a 12-year-old he displayed amazing strength. His mother advised us, 'Oh let him go, he'll cool down.' We acquiesced. Cursing and swearing, he tore down the path, pausing only to scoop up a handful of stones which he hurled at the minibus. 'I'm going to break every window in your house', he yelled back at me. Inside the house, we tried to explain what had happened.

5 The hate campaign. The eruption is followed by a campaign in which Daniel blackens our characters to anyone who will listen. He accuses us of being queers, of making money out of the project, of running lousy clubs, of interfering in other people's private affairs. At one stage,

he was even saying that our aim was to get kids put away.

6 Co-operation. The last stage involves Daniel making his peace. We never exclude him. Always try to greet him in the street. The time comes when he asks to return. A few days after the garden fork episode, he asked if his mum could wash the team's football shirts. We begin to enjoy his company and have some interesting conversations. He is enthusiastic and the cycle begins once more.

Within these cycles, of course, other events were occurring. He was making up bikes, coming to my house to make a go-kart, playing football and so on. He was also being drawn into delinquency. Other boys told us that he was into shoplifting and stealing bits from bikes. He told me he had stolen £500 worth of goods over the years, particularly bikes and electrical goods. Eventually, he was caught for a robbery and we accompanied him to court. At school, he was a regular attender while showing some behavioural problems.

Recently, another eruption occurred. Dave was taking football at which Daniel became increasingly aggressive. Not content with attacking other boys, he began to pinch their belongings. When Dave intervened, he flew into a violent rage and had to be taken home again. Daniel decided, thereafter, to leave all the clubs and ignored us in the streets. Now he is talking again but clearly the rift is the most serious yet.

What has the project done for Daniel? Very little. We have always allowed him to attend the clubs. After one exhausting session, a boy turned to me and asked, 'Bob, how can you go on putting up with Daniel?' I sometimes wondered. But we wanted to show him our concern by not excluding him while at the same time not condoning his excesses.

In addition, we tried to talk with him. While in the midst of a bad patch with Daniel, Dave said this:

I kept talking to him a lot and showing him what he was doing, almost analysing the things he was doing, because a lot of the time he tries to make whoever's trying to help him feel guilty. I was telling him that he was doing it, although he didn't listen and said 'I'm not listening'. . . but I found it important as well to tell him how much I cared for him as well as showing him all the bad.[14]

The salient point is that Daniel would not listen. He would not admit that he had problems or needed to change. The nurses were 'silly old bags' who wouldn't let you have fun. Teachers were 'not fair'. We 'picked on him'. Everyone was out of step except Daniel. We could not find any way of getting through to him.

Nor did we succeed in relating to his parents. I always had the impression of being kept at arm's length. Dave and I thought that the parents needed to control Daniel, to know what he was doing in the streets, to say at what time he should come in. But we lacked the skills to make any impact on them and I suspect that they had little regard for us.

Bert

Bert was never a regular at the clubs. He preferred to roam the town centre with other punks, to play the machines, to go to discos. He saw himself as a hard nut and a ladies' man. Still, we often chatted in the street and during his occasional visits to the clubs. His mother had separated from her husband some years previously. I admired her determination not only to keep her family together but to make sure that they lacked nothing materially. As Bert grew into his teens, she found him increasingly difficult to handle. Indeed, at one stage she had sent him back to his father. This proved no more successful and Bert was returned.

During these years Bert was drifting into delinquency. Truancy and school behaviour were further problems and he had already been transferred from one school to another. One day, the mum phoned me to say that Bert had been off school for a week and was refusing to go. I had a talk with him and the following Monday drove him to school. The school was not our local one and I went in with Bert so as to meet the teachers. The headteacher summoned Bert's tutor and two other teachers who began to bombard him with questions and telling-offs. Eventually, he broke down and wept. I took him outside and walked around for a bit. I almost regretted taking him back.

There followed a period of intermittent attendance. Sometimes he would phone to say he just could not face school. I would let him stay with us for the morning on condition that he attended in the afternoon. He was caned at school but this had little lasting effect. He hated the humiliation of looking inferior at subjects he could not grasp, he could not tolerate being ordered about, he would sometimes be disruptive in order to be kicked out. I talked with him and his mum about a 'Truancy School' in the town. I thought that he might respond to a more relaxed atmosphere. However, the headteacher had strong doubts about the quality of this school so I did not pursue the matter.

Bert was now summoned to an Educational Tribunal which referred him to the Child Guidance Clinic. Here the psychiatrist found him so uncommunicative that nothing could be suggested. Meanwhile, Bert had committed a break-in. I accompanied him to court and spoke for him. He was placed under the supervision of a probation officer and a condition made that he attend school regularly.

A new school year started. Bert was involved in some fighting in the street. Once his mother phoned me to say that Bert was refusing to go to school because she would not give him the money to purchase a new pair of boots. I went round and his grunting response was, 'If she won't do anything for me, I won't for her.' Between us, Dave and I managed to get him back to school for a few days. Having persuaded him to attend, the school decided to suspend him because of his defiance and aggression. He was allowed back but suspended again. Further, he was not turning up for his probation appointments. Next, his mum phoned to say that he was not sleeping at home. He would come in for a meal and then leave, not saying where he was going. At her request, I informed the probation officer.

Two days later, on a Sunday evening, the police phoned to say that Bert had been picked up sleeping rough. He refused to go home and the police reluctantly were having to keep him at the police station. Bert had asked the police to contact me. I informed his mum and went to see him. He was half enjoying the image of a hard man picked up by the police, half showing the fear of a boy. Subsequently, the probation officer took him back to court where a care order was made. He was transported to a community school where Dave and I would take his mum to see him. Bert absconded a number of times but was eventually allowed to return home while he spent his last year at school. Where? At the 'Truancy School'.

We were pleased that Bert was back in the community. Yet, in retrospect, I felt that his removal could have been avoided by better work on my behalf. In particular, I made a mistake not to push for a transfer to the 'Truancy School' at an earlier stage.

SOME LIGHT

Fortunately, the disappointments can be set against those lads who appear to have straightened themselves out. I say 'appear' for anything can happen in the future. The next two examples are of boys who went through stages of delinquency, deceit and misbehaviour and yet now seem to have stabilized. We have known them both for over three years.

Adam

Adam often regards himself as the new Elvis Presley. Even when we first knew him when he was 13 (he is now 17-years-old) he would grease his hair into the style of the American rock idol.

His father left home some years ago. Adam and his brothers and sisters have been brought up by their mum. She worked hard at a part-time job, but found Adam a handful, particularly as he developed into a well-built and powerful teenager.

A founder member of the youth club, Adam was not adept at outdoor ball games, but became an enthusiastic darts and snooker player. The club provided a much needed outlet, for he never had the money to enjoy activities in the town centre, while he was reluctant to stay indoors.

One morning, his mum knocked at my door, 'Bob, I want to see you about those ferrets.' For a minute I was taken aback thinking that she had mistaken our guinea pigs (whose babies needed homes) for a different species. Then I recalled some neighbourhood talk about ferrets which I had not taken very seriously. 'The Case of the Missing Ferrets', I entitled it as I put on my Sherlock Holman guise. In fact, I was wrong to treat it so lightly. The ferrets were prized animals used to hunt rabbits which provided good meat for eating. Two had been taken from a house and Adam was one of the boys under suspicion. His mum also poured out her troubles about coping financially, about Adam's dislike of school and his refusal to do anything she asked, from washing his neck to going to bed. It was the first of many calls from mum.

I asked Adam to see me. In the company of another boy, he had nicked the ferrets and by this time the irate owner had summoned the police. However, it was smoothed over without a prosecution. He began to call regularly. At the same time, mum was frequently complaining to me about his behaviour. She had heard that he was into glue sniffing. I tackled Adam about it in the street and persuaded him to hand over the glue which I then poured down a drainhole. The indignant Adam promptly asked me to pay for it. The next trauma occurred when mum arrived to say that her watch was missing while Adam now possessed a bike. I saw him and at first he angrily denied his mother's insinuations. I took the opportunity to talk about the nature of our growing friendship, about my desire to help him, about the confidences I would keep and the trust we would have to have in each other. He came several times that day and eventually told me the truth. He had exchanged the watch for the bike and now did not know how to get out of the mess. Together we went to see the bike owner and retrieved the watch. His mum, relieved to have back the watch, agreed to say no more on the subject.

I did not want our relationship to be just a response to crises, so it was fortunate that the Wiley Group commenced at this time and Adam came along. Here we saw more of each other in a relaxed setting. Interestingly, he turned out to be its most articulate member, always entertaining us with his views and personal experiences on any subject from vandalism to truancy.

Now aged 14, Adam went through a period of about nine months when delinquency threatened to get a hold on his life. He was into both local nicking and shoplifting from the town centre. With another boy he broke into a garage and stole some property. He was also stealing items of clothing. He was then caught shoplifting from a large shop and given a warning. Eventually, he was taken to court and placed under a two-year Supervision Order with a requirement for Intermediate Treatment. Even so, he continued in the same way. Soon after the court appearance he was out shopping with my family when my wife thought she saw him shoplifting. Afterwards I tackled him and insisted on taking the stolen object back.

What were we doing during this period? Firstly, we were *talking*. Adam acknowledged his problem, his inability to resist temptation and usually came to see me when he committed offences. We tried to explore the reasons. The obvious one was that he was perennially hard up. We also wondered if he was modelling himself on his absent dad, who still lived in the same city. Adam had mixed feelings towards him. He blamed dad for leaving the family in the lurch in order to live with another woman. At the same time, he admired his dad's hardness and exploits, for he too had been in trouble with the police. Together we made some contact with dad. After initial enthusiasm, Adam cooled. I had the impression that he felt disappointed with his father.

Secondly, our home became *available* to him. He would come in to have a coffee, or wearing his studded belt and tight-fitting jeans to talk about Elvis. At times also he used our home as an escape from planned thefts or shoplifting expeditions.

Thirdly, *we saw his mother regularly*. She would pour out her worries about his late nights, his friendships and so on. While appreciating her fears, we encouraged her to respond more positively to him, to praise as well as to criticize. At least she took comfort from the fact that he spent so much time at the clubs.

Fourthly, he continued at the clubs and groups and identified himself with the project. The Social Services Department, which was in charge of his Supervision Order and Intermediate Treatment requirement, were content to play a secondary role leaving us to have most contact with him. In addition, they did pay for Adam to accompany the Senior Club on its annual holiday.

Just when it seemed that Adam would certainly return to court—and to a custodial sentence—he managed to stop stealing.

One contributing factor was that he obtained an evening washing-up job. He gained satisfaction both from talking about the work and from having some money at last. He also chummed up with an older youth club member who lived in the same street and proved a stabilizing factor. They had a common interest in motorbikes and Adam persuaded me to lend him £20 to buy an old banger which he would put in order. The arrangement was that Adam's employer at the cafe would pay me back each week. The agreement worked well but with the almost inevitable snag. He promised not to ride it on the road until he was 16. He succumbed and appeared on the doorstep accompanied by our local policeman. The advantage of knowing the community policeman now became evident. He was aware of Adam's struggle and let him off with a warning.

And that struggle was being won. Indeed, when one of his old partners in crime stole his dad's rent money, Adam declined to join him in a spending spree and instead persuaded the boy to come to me before too much had disappeared. On the other hand, school attendance and behaviour were deteriorating in the last year at school; Adam could not see the point of attending. His uncooperative behaviour resulted in him being kicked out for a while and sent to us. After another blow up with a teacher he walked out and made his way to our home. We persuaded him to attend school on the grounds that he was still under a Supervision Order and it was advisable not to rock the boat. None the less, we were prepared to allow him to spend time with us while away from school with genuine illness and injuries. Always liable to be clumsy he broke his ankle in a typical Adam fashion. Sitting with a group in the street, he saw a friend suddenly cut his wrist with a piece of glass after being rejected by a girlfriend. Adam leaped up to help, tripped over a brick and finished up in hospital. The positive pay off was that he could legitimately stay off school and spent time with the project.

Relationships at home were also up and down. At 11.30 p.m. one evening he knocked on the window. Following an argument, he refused to go home. Dave went to see his mum while I talked to Adam and eventually he returned. Her nagging which he resented so much was partly an expression of her caring. So was her worry that he would be unable to obtain a job when he left school. As this date approached, we sat down together and composed some letters applying for various posts. During the last term at school the Social Services Department handed Adam's supervision to a student social worker. The same student was coming to the Wiley Club to give instruction in making transistor radios. He got on well with Adam and was able to observe the struggle he had made to go straight. Consequently, the student went back to court and successfully applied for the Supervision Order to be ended. This vote of confidence was of great encouragement to Adam.

On leaving school, he found it difficult to obtain full-time employment. We scanned the papers, made phone calls, took him to interviews and at last a semi-skilled post was secured. The job, in a garage, was just right for him. He appreciated the status of a worker instead of a schoolboy. His mother welcomed the additional income into the home and was prepared to modify her criticisms. At the time of writing, he remains a regular and enthusiastic member of the clubs and a firm supporter of the project.

Kent

A police car was parked in the street. I was on my way to the shop and paused with the small knot of curious on-lookers. Suddenly the door of Kent's house burst open. A terrified Kent was dragged out by two burly policemen. They pushed him against the car and then, to our surprise, Kent started giggling. The policemen looked even more annoyed, shoved him into the car and drove off.

Kent was 15 at the time and was being brought up by his elderly aunt and uncle. He had attended the clubs for two years but we still hardly knew him. Extremely shy, easily embarrassed, he found it difficult to talk to adults. His reaction was to sit in complete silence and then break out into inappropriate grins and giggles. Such behaviour tended to infuriate teachers and police and resulted in a few thumps for Kent.

The offence for which I saw him apprehended concerned the theft of a valuable bike. He was fined heavily and took the brunt of the blame. However, it was clear that Kent tended to be used by other boys. He was anxious for friendships and would shoplift to please others. Next, he was involved in the fiddle over school dinner tickets and then in a theft of £15 (see p. 49).

During his last year at school, his truancy and lack of co-operation created conflict with teachers. Knowing of his involvement in the clubs, one teacher contacted me and I agreed to speak to Kent. The interview was hard work. Social workers are sometimes accused of saying nothing but 'hum', but here it was Kent's conversation which comprised 'Er', 'No' and a giggle. However, we began to see more of each other, partly as he was now chums with Wynn. Consequently, our conversations developed more content. Soon after, he turned up at our house in a truculent mood saying he was not going to school because he had been summoned to see the Deputy Head. Kent was unusually insistent and I could not persuade him to go back. I allowed him in the house on condition that I phoned the teacher. The latter was extremely helpful and explained that Kent was being defiant, not working and disturbing the class. He had told Kent to report to the Deputy Head after school in order to sort it out. By this time, Kent had shrivelled up and would not speak on the phone. None the less, it was agreed that after school, the teacher would see Kent at my house.

The interview with the teacher should have demonstrated to Kent that teachers were prepared to spend time and effort on him. His attendance did not markedly improve and at times we were taking him to school. Then Wynn came up with the suggestion that Kent should join him on the work experience placement. We agreed, but the placement failed, mainly because of my growing unwillingness to tolerate Kent. Whereas Wynn, for all his faults, was a hard worker, Kent's favourite occupation was to slump in the armchair. This laziness tended to annoy both Wynn and myself. Finally, I lost my cool and kicked him out. Dave Wiles, who had been out at the time, disagreed with my action and pointed out that I was more tolerant with other boys' failings. On reflection, I agreed; it also became clear that Dave was the one more likely to build up a relationship with Kent.

Thereafter, Dave spent much time trying to heal the breach

I had made. At this time, Dave described his involvement as follows:

> I can offer him my interest and I think I can offer him encouragement in the things he is good at in order to show him that there are other ways forward . . . . I want to stress that when he feels like nicking something or when he wants to skive off school, he can always come here. Maybe since the rift was caused and he was not allowed to carry on with the day release he seems to have springboarded away from us a bit and I don't want to give up on him.

Slowly, Dave built up a relationship. They began to talk—yes, he could talk—about his family, the members he no longer saw, school and the future. At this time, Kent also became a regular player in the football team and my communication with him began to revive.

In the spring of 1979, Kent left school and found great difficulty in finding employment. He was at a loose end for some months and spent more time with us. One day, I was visiting a seaside town to make arrangements for our forthcoming outing, so I invited Kent and another boy along for the ride. Once in the town, I went about my business and later returned to meet them. They were not there and after an hour, I walked with sinking heart to the Police Station.

'Yes, we have got two teenage boys. Shoplifting. And who are you sir?' asked the Police Desk Officer. I told him. 'Tell me, sir, one of these boys, is there something wrong with him, he keeps laughing?' I explained that Kent's giggling was and expression of anxiety, not cheekiness, but I was too late to save him from a belting from an infuriated policeman. Later I asked Kent if he wanted to lodge a complaint but, as he rightly said, 'Waste of time. My word against his.'

Once again, Kent had been drawn into a theft against his inclination. He was accused in court but the other lad, to his credit, took the blame and Kent was not convicted.

Meanwhile, Kent had got a job. He immediately purchased a motorbike on HP. Unfortunately, he could not cope with the machinery in his job and was sacked. More weeks of unemployment followed during which he was arrested for stealing a pair of secondhand motorbike gloves. Another job, another sacking. Kent was now close to Dave and told him all that was happening. He came along to help at the boys' Junior Club where he made a regular niche for himself. He obtained another job as a labourer. Then a bombshell. He went to court on his own. I was away and Dave was ill. The magistrates took a hard line and he was sentenced to three months at a Detention Centre. Fortunately, a technicality brought him back to court. He had not been offered the option of a solicitor. The solicitor who was obtained, knowing of our involvement, contacted me. I was horrified at the sentence, knowing what a Detention Centre would do to an introverted, anxiety prone youth like Kent. The solicitor got the case adjourned and one week later both Dave and I spoke on Kent's behalf in court. We explained the progress he was making, and, under questioning from the solicitor, assessed the likely effects of a custodial sentence. The magistrate reversed the earlier judgement and Kent was fined.

The relief of Kent (and of his aunt and uncle) was enormous. He had been terrified and shattered by his one day at Detention Centre. Our intervention became a turning point. He became a most regular caller at the house. When he locked himself out of his own home, he naturally came and stayed with us for an hour. He volunteered to put up some shelves in the shed we had erected to store the club's kit. He took seriously his duties at Junior Club. He came to tell us about work and about his motorbike crash. When Dave was ill again, he sat talking with him for hours. At times, we could not believe he was the same defiant, inarticulate youth who used to flop into a chair and refuse to move. At the time of writing, Kent has kept out of trouble and retained his job.

THE OTHERS

The accounts tell of only ten youngsters. In the twelve months October 1977 to October 1978, we had direct contact with 74 youngsters (52 boys and 22 girls). By direct contact, I exclude those whom we saw only at the clubs or in the streets. I mean those who came to our home, with whom we had personal conversations. Table 3 presents some additional material about these youngsters.

Table 3
Direct contacts with youngsters 1977–78

	No. of youngsters	In trouble with police		Known to truant	
		No.	%	No.	%
Boys	52	19	36.5	17	32.6
Girls	22	2	9.0	5	22.7
Totals	74	21	–	22	–

It can be seen that 36.5 per cent of the boys had committed an offence for which police action had been taken while 32.6 per cent had truanted to the extent that the education welfare officers had been called in. The percentages for the girls are much smaller although, it must be added, our information about them was less comprehensive than for the boys. It is worth noting, in addition, that 26.8 per cent of the boys and 59.1 percent of the girls came from one-parent families.

The project, then, was reaching a core of youngsters showing difficulties at school, at home or in the community at large. At this point, attention should also be drawn to the others. For included in the 74 are those who were not presenting difficulties and who do not feature in the accounts presented earlier. Yet they supported and contributed much to the project. For instance, Sam was a teenager who, apart from some motorbike offences, always kept straight. During the first three years he was a regular at Senior Club, captained the football team and supported all the project's activities. He was a stabilizing influence on some of the other lads and was always co-operative. Philip did get into some nasty fights at school and was suspended for a short period. But he rarely made trouble in the neighbourhood and, as a helper at Junior Club, could be depended upon to look after the cash and to undertake any task we asked of him. James was partially deaf and from a low-income family. He did miss some schooling because of his ear troubles and his behaviour at home sometimes brought forth complaints from his parents to us. But we never regarded these as serious. Often round my house, he appreciated a cup of tea and some company. He would arrive and announce, 'I've come to see you.' He was always the first to volunteer to deliver notes, distribute leaflets or collect jumble. Not least, there was a bevy of younger boys always calling to talk about the clubs. Four or five always came at teatime on Sundays in order to scoff biscuits and watch TV before accompanying us to our local church. These, and others like them, were an important part of the project. They enjoyed the contacts with us, the games, the clubs and the holidays. Their presence meant that the project never became regarded as just a place for delinquents or truants. They provided a balance and served to help other members as well as themselves.

ADVANTAGES IN WORKING WITH YOUNGSTERS

The basis of the Edgetown Project was that its workers lived by the council estate, so that they became part of the community. Its approach was to work through clubs, groups and individuals. The approach had many limitations, as will be mentioned later, but here it is appropriate to list the advantages that its basis and approach gave to working with youngsters.

Firstly, we were *available when the youngsters wanted us*. Obviously much of the time they came just because they were at a loose end. More important, the home was a place where they could come immediately to blow up, to find shelter, to calm down. For instance, two teenagers living together had a violent row resulting in the boy slinging a chair through a mirror. The girl, who had already been in public care, ran out and came to our home where she could find safety and weep about what was happening. No other friends or relatives in the area, there was no where else to where she could have fled. Again, a teenage boy on the run from the police, with no money and no shelter, knocked on our door. We took him in for a meal and encouraged him to let us phone the authorities. Other boys have called in when sacked from their jobs. Youngsters have rushed down after rows with parents or after fights with each other. If, as explained earlier, delinquent acts are sometimes associated with feelings of aggression, then the home may have served as a kind of cooler where anger could be talked out instead of expressed in some unsocial form.[15]

But youngsters do not only come in times of anger, they have knocked when in despair, depression or confusion.

Availability also meant that they could call in order to give or contribute. A delinquent teenager, to whom I felt I was not getting through, called one day and offered to teach me to fish and gave me a couple of booklets on the subject. We had chatted about fishing, one of his interests, and I admitted my own failures. He now called to do something for me. Similarly, boys have dropped in with toothbrush racks, made at school, with pies they have cooked at work, with rubber balls which they have found and thought could be used at the play scheme. At times they have come to wash the project's little minibus, to dig the garden or even to do the housework. We have formed close relationships with a number of youngsters and within such friendships it is important to be able to give as well as to receive.

Secondly, the proximity of the project to the estate means that we can *respond quickly*. Consider Kevin. A strong, tough teenager, at the age of 14 he was almost out of the control of his mother. One evening when father was on nights, she contacted me because he would not go to bed and was terrorizing his brother. I was able to quieten him down and get him to bed. Such instances were repeated and, when he was 16, I had to go to his home as his mother was fearful that he was going to beat her up. My intervention provided no long-term solution, but it had meant that peace was restored for a few days. Even these small gains would not have been possible unless I could have responded quickly.

Whenever a local resident called or phoned in a panic we would attempt to act the same day. One father, an isolated and withdrawn man, called in a panic one Sunday over his son. He could not tell how ill he was. I found the boy, sick, shaking and breathless and immediately dashed him to hospital. He had pneumonia. Similarly, Dave has been able to respond immediately to a family when the boy's truancy and defiance provoked violence from the father and much anxiety in the mother.

Thirdly, the nearness to local people enabled us to acquire *much knowledge about residents*. In some weeks over 200 youngsters were seen at the clubs. I recorded that on one day

I might hold conversations with over 20 adults and children just by walking around the streets and shop. Such information can be invaluable when dealing with individual youngsters. For instance, one Friday evening a 16-year-old girl, Marlene, arrived in tears declaring that she would not return home, that her mother was beating her and that she was being made to stay in all the time. She was already on probation for theft and asked that she be taken into care or taken to the Police Station. At 5.30 p.m. I could not get a reply from Probation or Social Services Department. Having seen the girl's behaviour over some years, I knew I was receiving a one-sided picture and guessed that she was over-reacting. We talked further and the real disagreement emerged as her mother's dislike of her 23-year-old boyfriend. The mother had never met him but was accusing the girl of having sex with him. I asked Marlene to bring Joe round. We all talked and eventually agreed that the most sensible action was for mother to meet him. I then went to speak to mum. Already knowing her, I was not surprised to find that she was trying to curb the late nights Marlene was keeping and was worried that she might be sleeping around. She had cuffed Marlene but not beaten her (having seen Marlene in a temper, I could not imagine anyone beating her). Mother agreed to accompany me and so met Joe. A sensible discussion ensured about sex, drinking and staying out. Eventually, Marlene agreed to go home while mother said how relieved she was to have met Joe. Again, the relationship difficulty within the family was not solved but our knowledge about Marlene, mum and Joe did enable one crisis to be sorted out without resorting to the police or the statutory bodies.

Fourthly, the location gave a *closeness to what was happening*. On occasions, I arrived as one boy was beating up another in the street or as a father was kicking his son out. I was close by when a 13-year-old had his leg ripped open by the chain of a moped. Consequently, I was able to rush him to hospital and stay by him while he had a skin graft. The closeness also made us useful to the schools. The junior school has used Dave to look after a class or to provide transport for outings. Teachers at the comprehensive have brought unruly boys to our doorsteps or phoned to ask about missing boys.

Fifthly, the nature of the project meant that frequent contact was had with youngsters *over a long period of time*. Sometimes, years elapsed before youngsters had the confidence to talk about what was bothering them. A 14-year-old girl, with whom I had often conversed at superficial level, drew me aside to talk about her unhappiness when her divorced mother was going to marry again. Again, I was driving home three teenage girls, all long-established members of the club. They were all in similar predicaments and wanted to talk—they were all living with stepfathers and wanted to know about their real fathers. A teenager, very upset by his father's progressive illness, took two years before he could discuss with us the genetic implications for himself. While door-knocking at the start of the project, I came across a boy being raised by grandparents. I never seemed able to get near but now, after three years, he has started coming to our activities.

Sixthly, the project's involvement in clubs, holidays, groups, as well as individual counselling, meant that it had a *range of options to offer youngsters* who were in need. Making initial contact with a suspicious youngster might best be done by drawing him into the football team. The promotion of a boy's self-confidence might be engendered by giving him responsibility at one of the clubs. Youngsters can be embraced within small groups or have a close individual relationship.

I have formerly worked as a child care officer for a local authority and remain convinced that council social workers, backed by their resources and legislative powers, provide an essential service. None the less, I believe that small projects, such as the one described here, can offer something extra to youngsters. Being on the spot, the community social workers are available when youngsters need them—and this often seems to be in the evenings or at weekends. They can respond quickly, for they do not have to be reached by the receptionist and via engaged telephones and do not have to travel many miles to make contact. They gain an intensive knowledge of the neighbourhood, for it's where they live, where their own children go to school, where their children make friends, where they do the shopping. Local authority social workers covering much larger areas cannot possibly obtain the same knowledge.

Lastly, the community social workers not only have a range of options but actually attend the options themselves. A local authority social worker may advise a boy to join a youth club, whereas the community social worker may be able to take him to a club which he runs. Of course, the Edgetown Project could not and should not replace Social Services Departments, but if they have advantages in working with youngsters, then possibly something may be learnt from them.

4 The Parents

'It's the kids that count'

The project emphasized working directly with youngsters and during the first three years youngsters called at the home far more frequently than adults. Yet obviously, if a major aim was to help children remain within their own families, the latter could not be neglected. Thus, by contrast, adults — and the term refers usually to local parents — were visited in their own homes by the project workers more frequently than the youngsters. This chapter will describe how the project attempted to help parents and narrates four examples of work with parents. Initially, however, it will quantify the contacts made with them. The number of and reasons for the calls from and visits to adults can be seen in tables 4 and 5.

WHY THE PARENTS WERE SEEN

During the initial three years local adults called or were called upon 1,300 times. What were the main reasons? A look at tables 4 and 5 enables the following divisions to be made.

Clubs and Holidays
One of the objectives of the project was to provide youth facilities on the estate. The parents took an interest, some offered their help and, of course, they were visited to discuss their own children going on a club holiday. Thus, 19.7 per cent of the calls from and 6.2 per cent of the visits to parents concerned the clubs. Further, within the visits 14.6 per cent were about the outings and holidays and another 6.3 per cent

Table 4
Calls from parents to home in three-year period

| | No. of calls 406* |
| | No. of persons 471 |

	No.	%		No.	%
Club matter	80	19.7	Custody	22	5.4
For company	80	19.7	Martial disharmony	20	4.9
Financial difficulty	49	12.0	Crisis	16	3.9
Child care	31	7.6	To refer others	14	3.4
Prevention	29	7.1	Other	40	9.8
Accommodation	25	6.1			

* Of these calls 196 were made by a man; 185 by a woman; and 25 by a man and a woman together.

Table 5
Visits to or accompanying parents in three-year period

	No. of visits 894				
	No.	%		No.	%
Prevention	185	20.6	Club matter	56	6.2
Outings and holidays	131	14.6	Crisis	42	4.6
To give lifts	81	9.0	To give company	34	3.8
Adoption and fostering	66	7.3	Accommodation	30	3.3
Financial difficulties	64	7.1	Custody	20	2.2
Chid care	60	6.7	Other	68	7.6
To arrange play scheme	57	6.3			

about the parents' part in running the summer play scheme. Thus, parents were not contacted just because of personal problems. This important point will be taken up again towards the end of the chapter.

Prevention
In one sense it could be argued that every call and visit was about prevention because a major objective was to stop children needlessly leaving their families. Thus, even a visit to ask a mum to make the tea at the play scheme could be so defined. But, in fact, only a minority of parents were under strain so serious that a break-up seemed imminent. Work with this

number was termed preventive. This core of parents accounted for 20.6 per cent of all visits and 7.1 per cent of calls at the home. In addition, it was among these families that the crises tended to occur. By crisis is meant a difficulty of such proportions that we had to take immediate action. Examples are of a co-habitee threatening to kill the children, a walk-out by a parent, the kicking out of a child or the taking of an overdose. Fortunately, crises took up only 3.9 per cent of calls and 4.6 per cent of visits. None the less, this total of 58 calls and visits was quite enough, thank you.

To put prevention into perspective, in the one year 1977–78, contact was had with 45 local families. Of these, preventive work was undertaken with 12. Of the 45, 15 (33 per cent) were one-parent families. In addition, a limited number of visits were made to the elderly and single people.

Company
19.7 per cent of calls and 3.8 per cent of visits I have termed 'for company'. The term is not satisfactory for it covered a wide range. Within it are included a parent who might just drop in for a chat, a lone father who wants a man-to-man talk about doing a woman's job — bringing up kids — and an un supported mother who is desparately lonely and wants to talk with someone. The calls had no specific reason, like money shortage or child behaviour, but sprang from a more general need for support and friendship.

Financial Difficulties
Of all calls to my home 12.0 per cent, and 7.1 per cent of visits, concerned material problems. Obviously a modest project with no premises and whose income amounted to the workers' salaries and a few hundred pounds for running costs could not be regarded as a relief-giving agency. Yet material problems amonst residents loomed large and we encountered them on many occasions. For not only were there the times when people approached us, but the lack of money could be seen in families' difficulties in paying for the holidays and outings organized by the clubs.

Some residents on the estate were comfortably placed. But many found life a financial struggle. Three groups seemed particularly vulnerable. Those families dependent upon social security had enough to buy food and pay the rent, but could be knocked sideways by a high fuel bill or the need to buy their child a new pair of shoes. One-parent families were even more at risk. As the government's own *Family Expenditure Survey* for 1977 pointed out, such families on average receive less than half the income of a two-parent family though they have the same number of children to support.[16] Even some working parents could be in difficulties if in low-paid jobs such as warehousemen, cleaners and council manual workers.

Many, if not most, of the schoolchildren we work with were in receipt of free school meals. Low incomes were not unusual. To make matters worse, the council itself admitted that its rents were amongst the highest in the country. To this must be added the effects of inflation on the costs of keeping children. As a recent study has shown, these costs weigh particularly heavy on low-income families.[17] Such a family in Edgetown could be in distress if, for instance, faced with the following:

1 A child starting at secondary school with the cost of new school outfits being (in 1978) about £58.
2 The older child wanting to go on the youth club September holiday costing £25.
3 The teenage boy being fined £40 for shoplifting.

Thus, financial difficulties were not uncommon and not unexpected. Parents have come to the home with problems of the following kind. A couple called a few days before Christmas very distressed because having paid their bills they had no money at all to buy presents for their children. I have seen a man almost in tears as he was unable to afford the bus fares to visit his children who lived with his separated wife some miles away. A wife arrived tearfully showing me a bailiff's warrant resulting from the non-payment of rates. Families have knocked with no money to buy food for the weekend. I've known boys ashamed to go to school wearing shoes with great holes in. These are not typical cases and they must be set beside those parents, with children now at work, who can cope with no bother. None the less, some families were on the breadline. Even then they did not necessarily seek help. I recall a man who could not afford a suit for his mother's funeral. He regretted but just accepted the fact. I'm close to a woman who survives by scrubbing floors. She never asks for financial aid. But, at times, other families were so desperate that they took their material problems to the project.

Child Care Problems
This was behind 7.6 per cent of the adult calls and 6.7 per cent of the visits. Apart from concern over their children's delinquency, parents also wanted to discuss their emotional and behavioural problems. For instance, a woman asked me to call and I found her weeping over the disobedience and cheekiness of her teenage daughter. A man knocked, feeling shaken at the discovery that his seven-year-old child was a shoplifter. A woman was similarly upset when her girl staggered in drunk. Another mother was worried that a 12 year old was still wetting the bed. A couple complained that their son was hitting his sisters, staying out late and refusing to wash. A mum was disturbed when her daughter began knocking around with a married man.

To Give Lifts
Of the external contacts with parents 9.0 per cent were in order to give them a lift in the car. On an isolated estate, travel could be difficult. Thus lifts were often provided to take mothers — usually accompanied by small children — to the doctors, to the dentists and hospital. In an emergency, they would be taken to the chemists or to help a relative who was ill.

Adoption and Fostering
As an employee of the Church of England Children's Society, I acted to assess potential adopters, to make adoption placements and to help adoptions under strain in the Edgetown vicinity. During the three years, I also placed two children in foster homes. Together, the adoption and foster cases took up 7.3 per cent of the visits.

Accommodation
Of the calls to our house 6.1 per cent, and 3.3 per cent of

visits, concerned housing difficulties. For example, a woman, her co-habitee and children had moved in to her mother's. The resulting overcrowding caused tensions and we were asked to help. Occasionally, a young mother-to-be sought our advice about where to live once the baby was born. Parents also come to discuss dampness, overcrowding and eviction threats.

Custody
Divorces and separations can lead to battles over which parent has custody of the children and what degree of access should be allowed. 5.4 per cent of calls and 2.2 per cent of visits were with local people facing custody issues in the courts.

Marital Disharmony
Of calls to the home 4.9 per cent were from residents experiencing marriage problems. One woman frequently called while her husband was carrying on with another woman. A man always came when his marriage was under strain. At times, near to breaking point, he would implore me for advice as to what he could do.

Refer Others
Of all the calls 3.4 per cent were from residents wanting to report other people. Sometimes they were worried that children were being abused. At other times, their concern was for friends and neighbours experiencing difficulties and strain.

THE HELP WE OFFERED

Hopefully, the clubs and our involvement with the youngsters was of help to parents. It was certainly appreciated by them. In addition, we tried to respond to the kinds of problems they brought to us. In recent years, various schools or theories of social work intervention have been published. Our approach was not based on any of these or indeed on any theoretical basis. It was straightforward but very unsophisticated. The main elements were as follows.

Modifying Financial Problems

When residents arrived with severe money problems our initial approach was to go over their income and expenditure just to see what was happening to the cash. Often, the families were very hard put to make ends meet and thus we did not delve into explanations of why they could not cope, unless for instance one partner though the other was spending too much on booze, gaming machines or bingo. But this was rarely the case. More frequently, careful people could not meet unexpectedly large bills or the need to buy essential items.

The families under greatest stress were those surviving on means tested incomes, in particular supplementary benefit. Here we could be of immediate service by working out what they should be or could be receiving. Thus, I went with one man to the social security officer and corrected a mistake whereby he was receiving £5 a week less than his dues. In another case, the Supplementary Benefit Commission agreed to pay a family an extra £4 a month until after their outstanding debt on a cooker was paid. Cash for clothing, cooking and heating was obtained via Exceptional Needs Payments and Exceptional Circumstances Additions. Help was also given in applying for rebate for rates and fuel bills. Milk tokens were obtained for one lone mother. These increases did not solve financial problems but they did ease them.

Sometimes a financial crisis arose so severe that eviction was threatened. Then we have supported the residents as they negotiated with the council — or in one case with a building society — to make arrangements for reducing the arrears in future weeks.

The project had little money of its own but did have a small fund made up of profits from jumble sales and cafes. At times, this could be drawn upon to pay for youngsters who otherwise would not have been able to join our holidays. Similarly, we built up a stock of secondhand clothes, plimsolls and, sometimes, furniture which could be used.

As well as drawing upon the Supplementary Benefits Commission, negotiating with the Housing Department and using the project's own meagre funds, material help could sometimes be obtained via the WRVS, the local Social Services Department and small local charities. Once these channels were exhausted, I was sometimes prepared — although it goes against textbook social work — to use my own possessions. Small amounts of money would be lent out until the next giro or wage packet arrived. We gave a handicapped man some money to stop his telephone being cut off. Up to £30 was lent (and usually returned) to enable families to avoid having the gas or electricity cut off. Only once did recourse have to be made to the Social Services Emergency Team. Of course, these puny efforts could not provide an adequate financial income. At best, they enabled parents to survive one period of crisis.

Practical Help

Being on the spot and meeting people everyday, we were well placed to offer practical help. The small minibus, known as 'the van', was particularly useful. Dave used it to move people and their belongings from house to house. As mentioned, lifts were also given. Few people possessed cars and so turned to ask us for transport when John got hit in the head by an air gun pellet, or mum fell ill or Sid was run over. It was said that we had a season ticket to the hospital. Again, the van was invaluable when a man, who had just lost the custody of his children, had to leave the council house to be replaced by his wife. We toured the city looking for digs for him.

Occasionally, we looked after other people's children. Examples were when a wife was visiting her bloke in prison, when a lone mother had to attend a court hearing or when a husband and wife both had to work on the same evening. Early on, I was prepared to recommend certain teenagers as baby-sitters. Then, one set of parents returned early to find the teenage girl I had recommended in a state of undress — and she was not alone! Collapse of baby-sitting service.

Lone mothers sometimes asked me for help with broken appliances. I have cheerfully mended plugs and bikes but was usually defeated by broken TVs, and electric cookers which had blown up.

Not least, we have been a depot for lending items to neighbours. The iron, toilet rolls, hose pipe, rover point, fork, lawn mower, hoover, TV set, light bulbs, typewriter, soap, notepaper and cooking dishes all spring to mind.

Practical aid of this nature was small but tangible. It was usually much appreciated and promoted a friendly spirit between us.

Advice

A number of parents also came to us for advice when faced with official letters or legal proceedings. A man, protesting angrily, brought a letter which he thought was saying he could no longer receive social security. In fact, it informed him that his national insurance benefits were exhausted but that he could now receive supplementary benefit. We have also given advice on tax returns, divorce proceedings, separations and obtaining maintenance.

Apart from juvenile delinquency, the legal issue which came to us most often concerned the custody of and access to children. Initially, we recommended a solicitor to the parent. Thereafter, we would attempt to interpret the solicitors' letters and give our views on what line to take in court. After the custody and access orders were made, the parents were still likely to seek our advice on what effect their ex-spouse's access was having on the children, would it harm them to go on holiday together, could access arrangements be altered, and so on.

Accompanying

Sometimes advice was not enough and parents requested our presence when they went to an official appointment. Five examples will illustrate this form of help. Firstly, Dave went a number of times with families to help them state their case to the Housing Department. Secondly, a lone mum, bringing up four children, was charged with defrauding the Supplementary Benefits Commission of £10. Almost overcome with shame and fear — the official who called on her had hinted that she could be sent to prison — she asked me to accompany her to court. I went and spoke for her. She was fined. Thirdly, I attended court with a mother when her divorce was made absolute. Her history had been unstable but the judge awarded her custody of the children and indicated that his decision was much influenced by the support she was now receiving from the project. Fourthly, a mother was having difficulty in receiving any financial support for herself and children from her ex-husband. She found it difficult to cope with officials and was very hard of hearing. Consequently, I went with her to court when a maintenance order was made and again on subsequent occasions when the man was in arrears and asked for a reduction. Fifthly, a father, with a previous record, went to court on a serious theft charge. He asked me to go with him. I also spoke on his behalf emphasizing the likely effects of a prison sentence on his young and large family. He received a suspended sentence.

Counselling

Parents often called with anxieties about their children or their marriages, and sometimes came in deep distress. The help offered could not be deemed as therapy. We did not try to see the connection between the parents' present difficulties and their own childhoods. Dave and I would not claim to possess sufficient skills to undertake such psychological probing. Our lack of expertise meant that our approach had to be much more limited and straightforward. I call it 'counselling' which contained three major elements — comforting, listening and guiding.

One Saturday evening, I returned home having taken 20 boys out for the day. An urgent message took me round to a

divorced mother. Her former husband, who had limited access to the children, had been late in bringing the boys home. An argument developed in which he threatened to take them for the summer holidays and, indeed, to challenge her custody. To lose her children to what she considered his 'evil influence' was the mother's greatest fear. I just sat and comforted her. I went over her successful battles to overcome her past fears and anxieties. Given her husband's circumstances, I emphasized that he was unlikely to ask for a change in custody. She felt better and I left.

Evening. A man at the door. He had often been to discuss his marriage. Once he'd arrived after his wife had locked him out and would not let him in. Once he had dressed his two children (by a previous marriage) and called to ask me whether he should leave for good. This time they had been quarrelling over money and care of the children. He wanted to talk about the unfairness of it all, about all he did for her and all her faults. My role was mainly to listen along with a few questions and comments. This prolonged session enabled him to take stock and eventually to return home.

Just after lunch time. The phone went and Betty asked if she could call. Her son was truanting, cheeking her and being insolent to her husband (his stepfather). The latter had lashed out in a rage and marked the boy. I suggested ways in which husband and son might do activities together and how the subject of his real father might be broached. In short, I tried to offer some guidance. An intelligent and articulate woman, Betty was able to sort out the advice which seemed most useful.

Financial aid, practical help, advice, accompanying and counselling were the most common means we employed with the parents. Obviously our limited skills and small resources could not hope to create profound changes in parental behaviour. Our intention, at best, was to enable some families to survive difficult patches and to cope more happily with their children.

FOUR PARENTS

The tables revealed that 'prevention' took up a substantial

number of visits and calls. Four narratives will now be presented about parents whose families seemed close to break-ups or whose family circumstances were so under strain that the children might be harmed. With each family we tried to use the means of help just listed in order to relieve the pressures.

Brian

'Come in. You're just the man I wanted to see. Are you the bloke who put this note through the door?'

It was the early days of door-knocking. My practice was to drop in a letter explaining the project and then knock at the door a day or two later. A slim, dark-haired young man now invited me in saying it was remarkable that I should turn up just at this moment.

Brian Harrop came from a broken home himself and had spent part of his childhood in a children's home. He married, obtained a council house, had a couple of children and settled down with a steady job as a lorry driver. While both children were still young, his wife, Anne, had an affair with another man. Eventually, she went to live with him but visited the children. She dropped hints that, once she and her lover found suitable accommodation, they would claim the young ones. Brian was determined to keep the children. Part of his reason was that his wife had had other children by a previous marriage and subsequently relinquished their care. He anticipated that she would wax hot and cold and the youngsters would be shuttled around. The main reason, though, was his own love for them. When the wife deserted, he gave up his job and stayed at home. He found it difficult to adjust to a social security income and ran up considerable rent arrears. He then received a letter from the court welfare officer saying he would be calling to compile a report as Mrs Harrop had applied for the custody of the children. The day the letter arrived, I also knocked on the door.

I saw a great deal of Brian during the next few weeks and got to know him and the children. He was anxious about the court welfare officer, wanting to know what he would be looking for and what questions he would ask. Brian was convinced that the court would be on the side of the mother. He had already contacted a solicitor but felt that he disapproved of fathers staying at home. He had discovered a letter from his wife to her lover's mother and wanted to know if this could be used as evidence of her adultery. We discussed his financial affairs with the result that he sold his car and began paying-off rent arrears. Most of all, he wanted to talk about Anne. He was still very fond of — if not in love with — his wife, yet also very bitter and hostile towards her. We mulled over his reactions if she asked to come back. Obviously the children were missing her. The two-year-old boy kept close to dad while the three-year-old girl was eating less and bed-wetting. However, going by her past history, Brian reasoned that, if Anne did return, she was likely to take off yet again.

In these early days, I was particularly concerned about the children. Brian's housekeeping and cooking was of a high standard. He was aware of the youngsters' needs for love and security but hostile to his wife seeing them 'too often'. Neighbours were very supportive of him and offered to baby-sit, to wash, etc. I also went to see the solicitor. He appeared to have accepted that a mother should have the children. I explained my view that Brian would probably provide a more stable home than his wife. The solicitor promised to pursue the case with greater enthusiasm.

A few months later, I attended court with Brian. Most of the negotiations occurred outside the court room between the two solicitors. Eventually it was agreed that Brian should have custody and his wife have 'reasonable access'.

The custody decision was a great relief to Brian. He grew in confidence and the children were relaxed and apparently happy. I suggested that he put his daughter's name down for the local play group. However, he was still troubled by his wife's visits. He would complain to me that the children were unsettled by seeing her and expressed his fear that she would abscond with them. I explained the reasons why the court thought it in the children's emotional interests to see their mother. I also pointed out that his wife would be open to legal proceedings if she acted contrary to the courts directions.

Three months after the court hearing, Brian sent for me. He was more agitated than ever. His wife had complained that he was not looking after the children properly as their son was ill. A row had developed in which Brian ordered her out unless 'she wanted a punch in the teeth'. Anne then returned with her boyfriend who challenged Brian to a fight. As the boyfriend was built like an all-in wrestler, Brian wisely declined. The saddest part was that the children became upset during these scenes. By the time I arrived, Anne had gone but the wrestler was still hovering in the road. I advised Brian to record his version of the day for the benefit of his solicitor. The son was not seriously ill and we gave him some tablets to bring his temperature down. I urged Brian to keep cool during the visits in order not to upset the children. I then went outside and found (somewhat to my relief) that Anne's boyfriend had departed.

Over the next few months, Brian's life proceeded more smoothly. His wife's visits became more irregular and, according to local talk, her new liaison was not proceeding too well. I had advised Brian over his supplementary benefit and his financial affairs were now more stable. Then, late one summer's evening, a neighbour knocked to ask if I could visit Brian 'at once'. I arrived to find Anne sitting on the settee. She had quarrelled with Dick (her boyfriend) and was asking Brian if she could return. Brian just did not know what to do. It was the first time I had had a long conservation with Anne. Blonde and petite, her beauty was still evident in an anxious and strained face. She repeated that she had made a mistake, that, if Brian would take her back, she would stay in at nights and be a good wife and mother. However, it also transpired that Dick was sitting in a neighbour's house a few doors away to see if she was going home with him. Brian paced the floor, speaking to me as though to clear his own mind. He still had great feeling for Anne and knew that the children needed a mother. Brutally frank, he said aloud that he could never trust Anne not 'to have it off' with other men and that, if she came back, the pattern might be repeated to the detriment of the children. 'After all, it's the kids that count', he added. Anne hung her head and restrained the comments that must have jumped to her lips. She asked if she could just stay the night – in a separate room. Brian looked at me and I agreed that he could not be expected to make a decision just then so that there was some merit in waiting until the morning. Just then

Dick arrived at the gate. Anne went out asking me to see that
nothing happened to her. I gulped, nodded, and tried to adopt
the appearance of one who was a karate expert. Fortunately,
Dick was too taken up with verbally abusing Anne who had
told him the affair was over. Dick walked away with the parting shot, 'You can forget about your belongings but I'm
sending your dog back.' The time was now well past midnight
and we all agreed to rest.

Anne stayed the next day and then left. Brian had opted
for a stable life rather than an unsettled one with a woman
for whom he still had deep feelings. I felt concerned about
Anne and tried to get in touch. I heard that she returned
briefly to Dick and then headed back to her parents in the
north. In the ensuing years, she visited very occasionally.
Brian — who was in touch with Anne's mother — kept me
informed of her escapades. Anne now had former husbands
and children in London and the West Country and, according
to Brian, there could be more to follow. Once she threw
Brian into a panic by telling him that she was going to re-apply
for custody but nothing has happened.

These events occurred two—three years ago. Brian now
works part time and has a steady girlfriend. The children are
well and the bed-wetting stopped long ago. The girl — after
enjoying the play group — has settled down at school. I frequently see them. They are beautiful, healthy youngsters. I
rarely call in at Brian's but he supports our activities and I
see him in the street. He is a good and capable father who
needed support just for that period of crisis. I am convinced
that the right decision was made in giving him the custody.
But sometimes I recall that strained, hurt face of Anne's and
wonder what has happened to her.

Mr Sparrow
'Bob, can you come round? Dad's ever so ill.'

8 p.m. one evening, I hurried round to Rob Sparrow's
home. Mr Sparrow was a middle-aged, lone father. His wife
had left some years ago and Rob had devoted himself to
looking after the four children. He had given up work, partly
from choice, partly because of ill health. He was a capable
cook and kept the house and garden in good condition,

despite frequent troubles due to his illnesses and financial shortages.

When I arrived, Mr Sparrow was rolling on the floor in agony, complaining of stomach pains. I returned home to phone his doctor and, after some considerable delay, a locum arrived. After a quick examination, he reported that Mr Sparrow must enter hospital straight away for treatment for a stomach ulcer. Mr Sparrow promptly refused, 'I'm not leaving the kids. Last time I went away they went into care. They're not going into a home again.'

The children said nothing. They always seemed quiet, almost withdrawn children, and now they were reduced to a fearful silence. I asked about relatives who might help. No. I knew that Mr Sparrow was not popular in the area so I could not be sure that neighbours would help. I had a hurried conversation with the doctor and then said, 'Rob, you must go to hospital. I promise you that the children will stay here in your home.'

Mr Sparrow went into hospital. Dave and I then established a system of caring for the children. One of us would pop in early in the morning to ensure that they got up. We would return to see that they had gone to school. A neighbour agreed to meet the three youngest children at 4 p.m. and give them a snack. Dave or I would call at about 6 p.m., when the oldest boy would prepare a meal. Later we dropped in again to make sure the young ones were in bed. The scheme worked. The children were able to stay in their own home until dad returned. Even so, he did discharge himself earlier than was recommended.

Mr Sparrow would sometimes turn to the Social Services Department, especially when in financial difficulties, and we liaised with the social worker to avoid any overlap. He called on us when he wanted to discuss his personal worries. He seemed to find it helpful to talk about his police record, the reasons for his marriage break-up, and his worries about one of his sons who was 'backward'. As he had little close contact with neighbours, the opportunity to chat was important to him.

Over the initial two years of the project, three problems loomed large – girlfriend, money and kids. Mr Sparrow formed

a liaison with a married woman who moved in with her teenage son. While meeting some of his emotional needs, the new
relationship created other difficulties. The teenage boy was a
handful and did not always get on well with Rob's children.
Belinda, the girlfriend, tended to suffer from depression and
was twice prosecuted by the police for shoplifting. Not least,
the house became overcrowded. Rows developed and Belinda
took an overdose and was hospitalized. Mr Sparrow was very
shaken and, in his talks with me, said he now wanted Belinda
to go. Unfortunately, she had nowhere to go. A probation
officer who had been seeing Belinda since the shoplifting
tried to find digs but without success. These were trying days.
Mr Sparrow allowed her back after her period in hospital, but
she was still taking tranquillizers and spent much of the time
just sitting and staring into space. He was looking increasingly
haggard and ill. Eventually, she decided to return to her
husband. I had the sad task of transporting Belinda, son and
bags to where she came from.

Simultaneously, Mr Sparrow was finding it hard to cope on
his income from social security. I helped him write a letter
asking for a review of his disablement pension. I also made
small loans and was able to obtain some firewood when he
was completely broke. To make matters worse, he was nicked
for not having a TV licence. Together we wrote to the court
explaining his circumstances but he still received a heavy fine.
Its payment became a burden. For a year he did not pay,
partly because he lacked the money, partly because the
traumas with Belinda were occurring at the same time. Receiving an urgent message, I visited him to find the police had
delivered an arrest warrant for non-payment. I phoned the
police station but found them insisting that he pay or report
to the station where they would put him in the cells. I returned to Mr Sparrow and found him in an almost suicidal
mood — possibly he had even attempted to take his life. The
house was freezing. I managed to obtain some fuel and
persuaded him to go to the doctors. Between us we raised a
little cash and averted another court appearance.

With the police crisis over and Belinda gone, Mr Sparrow
gradually brightened. He cleared out some secondhand clothes
for me to give to people who needed them. He undertook

some part-time jobs, bought a snappy suit and began courting again. He was still troubled by ill health and frequently at the doctors and hospital. Twice more we kept an eye on the children. Once an anonymous caller reported to the Social Services Department that he was leaving the children unattended. The social worker contacted me and I assured her that Mr Sparrow's care of the children was satisfactory and, indeed, that he had made tremendous efforts not to neglect them.

Mr Sparrow's difficulties were further lightened when his boy left school and obtained employment. His eldest daughter began to blossom, joined the senior youth club, made more friends and came on the holiday. He decided he could work full time again and bravely took on a job as a manual worker. The financial struggle was thus eased. Today, ill health is still a problem but he is sticking at the job. I now see much less of him although we speak in the street. He has survived some nasty crises which, hopefully, will not return.

Thelma

'Just a housing problem.' A retired church social worker had phoned me about one of her former unmarried mothers. Thelma, she said, had contacted her about her housing conditions. She just needed help to negotiate with the Housing Department. That was my introduction to Thelma.

Thelma, then in her early 20s, had experienced a chequered childhood. She had alternated between her mother, an aunt and children's homes. She emerged as a tough fighter, subject to periods of depression. Striking rather than beautiful, she was never short of boyfriends whom she tended to find in the criminal fraternity. She later boasted, 'I've been with some of the toughest blokes in the city.' When I met her, she had had one child from an early liaison placed for adoption. She subsequently married and separated. Mick was born by another man and Tom by a third. She retained their care and was living in a council flat. Her current boyfriend stayed at weekends.

She eyed me up and down when I called. 'Sorry to keep you waiting, I thought you wanted the TV money.' I explained about the retired social worker. 'Oh, she's retired now. She arranged the adoption of my girl. Wish I'd had this little buggar adopted as well.' She pointed to Tom, a few months old, who was bawling away. She showed me the flat. It was certainly damp. I began to make friends with six-year-old Mick.

A couple of days later Thelma phoned. The ceiling had fallen in. I contacted the Housing Department who, within a few days, arranged a transfer to a council house. The move took Thelma somewhat outside of Edgetown but I decided to maintain contact as I felt concern for the children. Sure enough, the next day, in a snowstorm, Thelma phoned in tears. The gas was not working in the new house, the TV was broken, Tom would not stop crying and she wanted to get rid of him. I took them all to my house to thaw out, organized the gas man and a TV repair.

Over the following months my attention focused on Thelma's care of the children. She did love Mick and Tom and was a good housekeeper and cook. Indeed, she took a fierce pride in her standards for which she would often seek my approval. But, raising the children, she found it difficult to achieve the balance between indulgence and control. She would stuff them with sweets and then respond angrily when they kept asking for more. The problem was intensified by the intermittent pattern of relationships with men and financial difficulties. Soon after moving house, Thelma had finished with the man who had been coming at weekends. One day the door was opened by Ben who informed me he had moved in. As the pattern developed, I began to worry about the effects on the children. Permanently living on supplementary benefit, Thelma was on the breadline. Her blokes were usually unemployed and so did not improve matters. The anxiety of bills and her failure to achieve the kind of material standards she desired became another burden. Sometimes she would crack. The dolled-up, swinging mod who carefully stood in the position which revealed her figure to best advantage would be transformed into a hunched up, depressed, drawn-looking woman. Then she could hit out at anybody and everybody.

Twice in a week, Thelma smacked Tom hard. The baby was unwell and continually crying. Neighbours had complained. Thelma was fed up with staying in all the time. Ben had now cleared out. One evening, she was convinced that Tom was seriously ill and sent for an ambulance. In fact, he had no more than a heavy cold and conjunctivitis. The co-operative staff, seeing the state Thelma was in, were prepared to let Tom stay just to give her a break. A distant elderly relative of Thelma's lived in Edgetown and I asked her to take Mick for a few days. Thelma was delighted. She had let the housework go of late but now she started with renewed vigour. She re-arranged the furniture to give Tom more room to crawl around. Together we sorted out the gas and electricity bills. We found a secondhand washing machine. Thelma chatted up a local dad who plumbed it in. A new boyfriend, Wilbur, appeared for a brief period.

After a few days, Thelma received her two children back. I called frequently. We discussed the need to control the children without recourse to either bribery by sweets or hard smacking. The following weeks were amongst the smoothest we experienced. Then Thelma fell head-over-heels for Des. Wilbur got the boot and trauma moved in.

Des had just served another prison spell for armed robbery. He was well known in the area for his violence. Tall, strong and articulate, it was easy to see why Thelma had fallen for him. She was high at first and wanted people to see her by the side of this well-known figure. But a foretaste of life with Des came when he grabbed the social security money. He gave Thelma £3 for food and spent the rest on drink and fags. She was too frightened to remonstrate, frightened for herself and the children. She reported to me that Des had threatened to 'do' her and the kids if she tried to get rid of him. He said that if he did return to prison, it would be for something really serious. An indication of Des' control was the tattoos he made Thelma wear. She showed me her arms and other parts of her body covered with obscenities as well as 'property of Des'.

No doubt Thelma gained something from the relationship apart from the boost to her ego. I reckon she felt more for Des than for any of her other blokes. She accepted the slaps and the cuffs. She told me what was happening but begged me not to do anything in case Des took his revenge. But I felt she was cracking under the strain. Mick was whining constantly and competed with Des for her attention.

At this stage, I was following three lines. Firstly, I was checking that the children were actually being looked after.

Des wanted Thelma with him at the pub in the evening. He assured me that they always arranged baby-sitters but I was not convinced. At least once Mick had woke to find himself alone and wandered into the street. I began to drop in. Usually a baby-sitter was present. Once it was a young woman and a boyfriend who, it happened, was subsequently convicted for a child murder! Once, I had difficulty in getting a reply. Finally, a scantily dressed girl opened the downstairs window. I insisted on seeing the children (who were asleep) while she returned to her man on the settee. I was worried.

Secondly, I voiced my fears to Thelma and Des. There followed long discussions not only about the present but the past. Des had received psychiatric treatment in prison and was keen to trace Thelma's problems to her childhood. Des regarded me as a threat. Once he called me upstairs when I knocked and we conversed as he cuddled Thelma in bed. It was as though he was saying, 'she's mine'. Polite at first, the facade began to break as I expressed dissatisfaction with the care given to the children. At times, I felt real fear.

Thirdly, I contacted the Social Services Department. If a crisis arose I wanted their backing.

The phone woke me at 12.20 a.m. Thelma was in a phone box. I could not understand her garbled words but knew it was serious. When I arrived, she was slumped on the kitchen table. The children were still up. Mick turned to me, crying, 'Bob, I can't stand it. Take me away.'

I picked him up. Thelma explained the events. Some weeks before I had helped Thelma negotiate with the Supplementary Benefits Commission who had now sent a bed, cot and a giro for £70 for blankets and clothes. As soon as she cashed the giro, Des had taken most of the money and had been drinking heavily. Returning late that night, arguments and threats had ensued. Des had armed himself with the kitchen knives. When he went into the garden to cool down, she had run out and phoned me. I decided that it was not safe for the children to remain. We were about to leave when the door opened and Des staggered in, bottle in hand. I remember foolishly and inadequately thinking of nothing else to say except 'good morning'. However, I told him that I was not going to let the children stay. Des just continued drinking. Hastily packing a few clothes, we left. Thelma had the presence of mind to take the electricity meter as she left. She said there was about £52 in it.

Back at my home, we put the children to bed. We snatched a little sleep until Tom woke at 6.30 a.m. Thelma had gone. I guessed she was attempting to make peace with Des.

The next morning I took Mick to school where his headmaster and teacher reported that he was attention-seeking of adults but working well. My wife continued to look after Tom. Calling at Thelma's, I found she and Des at one together. Thelma claimed that everything was fine. Des had promised to give up drinking, to hand all the money to her and to be kind to the children. I still argued that the children should go into care until the home was safe. Des was not pleased with me and walked out of the room. Thelma insisted that everything was alright and she wanted the children home. I phoned the Social Services Department who felt they could do nothing at present unless Thelma consented. I took Mick and Tom back where Thelma and Des made a great fuss of them.

At this stage I was feeling unhappy. Not only was I worried about the safety of the children but I had botched up any relationship I had had with Des. I determined to talk with him but within a couple of days, Thelma again phoned – on a Saturday evening. She reported that she and Des had been arguing over money, that Des was getting aggressive and Mick kept crying. I visited. Des just walked out. Mick clung to me. Thelma had changed her attitude. She was willing to put up with Des but agreed to accompany me to the Social Services Department next week to discuss the children's safety.

At the Social Services Department, Thelma appeared weary. She now wanted the children to be removed until her home life was stabilized. She felt that Mick was most at risk as he 'gets on Des's nerves'. She now definitely wanted Des to go – he had struck her again in front of the children – but was too scared to say so. The Social Services Department efficiently located a foster home for Mick. It was possible for Mick to attend his usual school while Thelma could meet him each day in order to maintain contact. Afterwards, Thelma and I explained to Mick what would be happening.

Before the usual introductions between child and foster

home could be made, another incident occurred. Early one morning I was called to the police station. Des and Thelma had come to blows as a result of which Thelma had grabbed Mick and run out of the house. Fortunately, the police arrived at this point having been summoned by neighbours alarmed at the noise. Des now charged out carrying Tom, declaring he would cut him up. More police were summoned. Des was located. He assaulted one policeman before he was overcome. It was then realized that Des had hidden Tom and he would not say where. Eventually, the police undertook to take no further action if Des produced the baby. He agreed and led them to Tom — quite safe — dumped in a nearby car.

Despite the police assurance to Des, I felt angry that no further action had been taken. From the police station, I phoned the Social Services Department who agreed to act straight away. The council social worker joined me. The police inspector offered some of his men to accompany us but we felt they would only provoke Des. When we called, Des was cool and off-hand. He claimed that the police had blown up the situation, that Mick had not been upset and Tom in no danger. Thelma, by contrast, was literally shaking. Her eye was blackened, her face puffy. I said the children must go and she agreed. We took Tom to a foster home on the borders of Edgetown. Mick's prospective foster parents were away for a couple of days so he stayed with me until they were back.

During the next month, I saw Mick almost every day as I usually took Thelma to meet him from school. He settled well into the foster home but was worried that he might lose mum altogether. The kindly foster parents were in the process of adopting a baby and I had to explain to Mick that he was not being adopted. Mick also missed Tom, so, at times, we would all go to see him. Thelma found she missed the kids and wanted them back. She wanted Des to go but could not tell him so. The end came suddenly. Des found another woman and moved in with her, taking money from the electricity and TV meters as he left. Slighted by Des's desertion to another woman, Thelma reported the thefts to the police. She immediately regretted her action fearing that Des would cut her up. For some days she would not leave the house and asked for police protection. She now asked to have the children home.

They were in care under a voluntary agreement and were returned. Des did not return and Thelma attempted to pick up the pieces.

The following few months were peaceful compared with the above trauma. Thelma had been deeply affected by her relationship with Des and she went several months, as she put it, 'being good'. We had many talks about her past and the needs of the children. She even acknowledged the desirability of a settled home life. Thelma said that her aim was to give them a better life than her childhood. But towards the end of the year another man moved in. Bill had just received a suspended prison sentence. But he was a gentler character than Des and played with the children.

Mick was now nearly eight, Tom nearly two. Although performing well at school, Mick was in trouble in the neighbourhood. He was caught several times stealing sweets from the local shop. He was also becoming increasingly disobedient at home and was not past telling Thelma to 'f— off'. In return, she would threaten to have him sent away. As Tom became increasingly mobile and demanding at this time, Thelma's patience was often at breaking point. Financial problems added to the strains. Further negotiations with the Supplementary Benefits Commission resulted in Thelma receiving the long-term addition (and some back payments) to her weekly income, plus an extra heating allowance for Tom whose persistent chest weakness was causing some medical concern. Together we purchased a radiator and Thelma made several improvements to the home. She was always at her most cheerful and happiest when planning such improvements.

Unfortunately, other pressures were to be added. Thelma had been heavily fined for not possessing a TV licence. Now she was summoned to court for not paying the fine. Simultaneously, a heavy fuel bill dropped through the letter box. Bill had moved out. A feud developed between Thelma and another unsupported mother in the street. The latter was spreading rumours that Tom and Mick had fleas. Thelma's escapades meant that she was not popular. Local and neighbourhood hostility now accelerated. With little money, no boyfriend, unfriendly neighbours, just a few days before Christmas, Thelma took a handful of sleeping pills. A friend phoned to say that Thelma was asking for me. I rushed round, found her very drowsy and hastened her to hospital. Here she was pumped out and kept in for a day. She discharged herself as she'd been put in a ward with a lot of old people. She added, 'Mind you, that young doctor was nice. I fancy him.'

She picked herself up and bounced back. She sold her record player, paid the fine and we went out and bought some food for Christmas. As she stood there, half-flirting, half-arguing with the greengrocer over a sack of spuds, I could not help but admire her cheek and powers of recovery.

The Social Services Department had maintained an interest in Thelma and her children. Nationally, several cases of child abuse had hit the headlines and the local social work team were worried about the safety of Tom and Mick. Early in the new year, they called a case conference to which the health visitor, doctor and I were invited. The physical danger could come from two sources, it was considered. Thelma might crack under the strain and lash out. More likely was the threat of attack from the kind of men who drifted in and out. At this point, Thelma was in the midst of another affair. In addition, concern was expressed at the effect on the children of the multiple fathering and Thelma's child rearing methods. Yet it was agreed that Thelma loved the children and they wanted to be with her. Although Tom was not yet three, it was felt he would benefit from a place at the town's day nursery. Not only would he mix more with other children but Thelma would be placed under less pressure.

Thelma was delighted at the day nursery suggestion and accepted with speed. For a brief period, she took on a day-time job at the bingo hall. I tackled her again and again about the boyfriends. It was a touchy subject. As a worker for a voluntary society, I had no official right to call or advise. If she told me to clear off, I would go. Moreover, she had to be the keeper of her own morals. As she retorted, 'You can't expect me to live like a nun.' On the other hand, I was convinced that the ever-changing faces did have a detrimental effect on Tom and Mick.

And Mick's behaviour was a source of worry. The shop-lifting had recurred and Thelma was finding him difficult to control at home. Twice Mick did not come home from school. Thelma was frantic with worry and phoned me. Both times Mick had gone to play with friends. The school were also perceiving more problems, particularly in Mick's aggressive behaviour towards other children. The school referred him to the Child Guidance Clinic. Thelma welcomed the idea at first as she considered Mick did 'have a few screws loose'. However, both she and Mick disliked the visits, found them boring, and would not persevere. At the same time, I often saw Mick on his own, taking him out for drives or back to my house. We spoke about the stealing and cheekiness. Mick could verbalize about how he loved mum and how he hated sharing her with all the men who came. Once he suddenly asked me what would happen to him if mum died. I tried to be honest. Thelma had a married brother who sometimes took an interest. Or he might have to live with someone like the foster parents. I added that Thelma's death was not likely in the near future but wondered if he was really asking whether Thelma was going to go on looking after him. Mick realized, I went on, that mum sometimes found it difficult to look after him but I did know that she loved him very much.

Tom had taken to screaming in defiance. His time at the day nursery had been restricted by a number of children's illnesses. I called when he had measles. The latest boyfriend – the second that month – walked into the other room. Tom was very miserable, demanding constant attention. Thelma, also having problems with Mick that day, seemed at her wit's end. 'I'll kill him,' she screamed. We spoke about the kids' needs – for stability, love and control. We spoke about Thelma's similar needs.

A couple of days later, she phoned again. I called. Frustrated by Tom's screaming she had slapped him hard on his back and legs. Thelma said that she wanted the children to go into care again so she could have a break. I took the opportunity to discuss whether the children – or one of them – should stay permanently in care. Thelma said she had been thinking about that. She referred back to her first child whom she placed for adoption. She often thought about her but guessed she was having a better life than Tom or Mick. She thought she had had children too early. She had missed out being a teenager and now wanted to make up for it. She agreed that we should meet again with the Social Services Department.

Before we met with the Social Services Department, Thelma got unusually low. She made Mick take Tom out while she slept for hours. Twice she just walked about the city centre until the early hours of the morning, leaving the children in the care of Duane, her new co-habitee. We went together to the Social Services Department, who agreed to receive the children, with Thelma's consent, for up to a month and then to review the situation. Thelma and I explained to Mick and Tom what was happening and soon afterwards we placed them in the foster homes, although, unfortunately not in the same homes as before. Once again I transported Mick to school every day and ensured that he visited Tom.

Thelma was less keen to visit than before. She had now taken up with Duane's best friend and was into a pot-smoking, motorbike-riding set. She felt she was not fit to be a mother and did not want her kids to turn out like her. Suddenly she took off on the back of one of the motorbikes and was not seen for some weeks.

The Social Services Department did review the case and, in view of Thelma's behaviour, began to think in terms of long-term reception into care. I continued to visit the children but, as it seemed the local authority might be taking over permanently, began to cut down the visits just as the council social worker increased his contact. Moreover, the foster homes were some miles away from Edgetown and I wished to concentrate on the project area.

The children did well in the foster homes although Mick missed mum. Then mum returned. Refreshed and bouncy, she was the old Thelma. She began to visit the children and wanted them back. The local authority opposed. They were prepared to go to court and argue that Thelma's mode of life was such that she should not have the children. Then Thelma, as unpredictable as ever, got married. She settled down with a husband who had a job, stayed in at nights and redecorated the house. She claimed that her adolescence was over and insisted on having the children back. The local authority had to accept.

The few months up to the end of the third year of the

project, Thelma continued to cope with husband and children. She did have financial crises and called on the Social Services Department. Their social worker took the line that her days of dependency were over, that she had wanted the responsibilities and that now she could manage. It seemed to work. I called in occasionally being careful to point out my position. Thelma treated me like an old friend and took pride in showing me the house while making a few digs about my lack of faith in her. She said the kids were terrible but obviously didn't mean it.

Of course, the testing times are yet to come. Whether she can last with one man has yet to be proved. What effect all the changes have had on Tom and Mick can not yet be assessed. As far as the project is concerned, this dramatic case highlighted some of its strengths and limitations. The project's nearness to Thelma meant I could visit her intensely. At some periods, I was calling every day of the week. My home was available to give shelter to her and the children. We could be in touch with each other within a few minutes. Seeing her so often meant I witnessed her strengths as well as weaknesses. On the other hand, the project's limitations also stood out. I was disappointed that, for the second reception into care, it was not possible to find foster homes within the area so that the children could stay in the community they knew. It may have been that Thelma and Mick needed therapeutic help of the kind I was not skilled enough to offer. Again, Thelma may have been better helped by becoming part of a group of mothers from the estate. At this stage, I had not awarded time to developing such a group.

Mrs Weaver
'Is your mum in?'
  'What?'
  'Is you mum in?'
  'My mum died years ago.'
  It dawned on me, I had dropped a clanger. The slim, dark-haired girl whom I thought must be a teenage daughter was Mrs Weaver — mother of four.
  While door-knocking, people had told me about Mrs Weaver. She rarely mixed with neighbours and had not lived in the

road for long. But it was thought that her husband had left her and she was struggling with four young children. I had decided to call.

Mrs Weaver had heard of me through her children. She invited me in. The house was spotless. There was a marked lack of toys — whether through poverty or choice I could not yet tell. She was a shy woman who had not made friends in the street. She was pleased to tell someone about her troubles. There were four children, Willie (10), Dolly (7), Anne (3) and Bet (2). I expressed genuine surprise that she could have a child of 10. She blushed and told me that her first two children were the results of a liaison when she was in her teens. She had subsequently married George and had two more children. She added that Willie and Dolly thought George was their real father and she worried about how to tell them the truth.

George was a labourer, often out of work. Mrs Weaver said she had married him partly to find a home for herself and a father for the children. They quarrelled a lot and twice she had walked out. Now he had gone away to work at a seaside fairground. Neighbours knew about their arguments and she felt they talked a lot about her. George did not send enough money and the rent arrears were mounting. Anyway, she wasn't sure if she wanted him back. She wasn't sure if she could carry on at all and often just wanted to walk out.

Mrs Weaver was a lonely, hard-pressed mother. She was near to breaking point and she turned to me as a last hope. Financially, I could help by making small loans which she repaid when she drew her Family Allowance or when George sent something. We visited the WRVS and obtained some much-needed blankets and clothes. I was prepared to do a few jobs around the house such as mending a plug or fuse. Sometimes, the children came to play at my house in order to give her a break. She had a sister on the other side of town whom she rarely saw because of the expense of taking four children on the bus. Now I took them over once a week in the car.

Gradually, Mrs Weaver began to surface. She talked no more of walking out. She had a deep love for the children, took pride in their appearance and was ambitious for them to be well educated. She also talked much about her marriage. She realized that financially she would do as well – or better – to separate and draw social security. But there was more to it than that. She resented George's lack of interest in the home and family. She considered he would never be a good worker. At the same time, I saw that the marriage was not completely dead for she worried in case he was consorting with other women and was angry that he hardly ever wrote. George appeared to work seven days a week while trade was good and so was not coming home to visit. I argued that they must talk about their marriage and offered to take Mrs Weaver in the car to see him. She accepted. A neighbour agreed to look after Willie and Dolly when they came out of school, while Anne and Bet accompanied us.

After a 60-mile drive, we met in a seaside fish-and-chip shop. George seemed pleased to see his wife and two children. He didn't ask after Willie and Dolly. After half an hour and two fishy cups of tea, I left them together and explored a British seaside resort on a rainy day. Mrs Weaver considered the visit a success. They had had a straight talk and George wanted to come home once the season was over. But she wished he was more kind, more loving. I took her again, this time accompanied by all the children. Bet was sick a few times during the trip and Mrs Weaver became irritated. George took little notice of Willie and Dolly, a point his wife obviously resented.

A few days later, Willie asked me to call. Mrs Weaver was very low. George had sent no money. He hardly ever wrote. He – like men before – valued her for one thing only, her performance in bed. She threatened to kill herself, to abandon the children. She told me how she envied her sister who was divorced, had no children, and was enjoying a swinging life. She resented having children in her teens so that she had to become a mother before she finished her own childhood. We talked for a long time, about her expectations from marriage, about her hopes for the future, about the nature of happiness.

I took Mrs Weaver to see George a third time. A neighbour agreed to look after Anne and Bet while my wife, Annette, cared for Willie and Dolly after school. Mrs Weaver was able to spend a long period alone with George. Two weeks later,

she asked to see me again. She told me that a male friend of
her sisters had invited her out. They had gone dancing and he
had called the next day and taken her and the children out.
She had accepted because she had decided that her marriage
to George was over. I urged her not to make a hasty decision
and wondered if her attitude was swayed by an infatuation
for the new man.

During the following weeks, Mrs Weaver had long and
serious discussions with me. She had no friends in the neighbourhood and found her sister too frivolous to talk over the
kind of decisions she was making. She told me what the new
man did for her and compared him with George. She was
perceptive enough to see that the boyfriend could not be
assessed on a few evenings out. She ended this relationship
and then took up with another man, Andrew, also introduced
via her sister. The relationship blossomed. She was in love
with him. Andrew was no angel but he did have qualities of
kindness which she was seeking. Andrew called and stayed.
The hostility of neighbours was aroused, not so much because
Mrs Weaver was 'carrying on', but because she was doing it
while George was away. Such was Mrs Weaver's feelings for
Andrew that she was quite prepared to endure the taunts,
looks and sneers.

At this stage, I was probably the only adult in the area who
was talking to Mrs Weaver. I believe I was subject to some
criticism on the grounds that I was 'encouraging' her to
deceive George. Mrs Weaver asked me frankly to say what I
thought. I talked about the likely effects on the children. I
acknowledged her estimate that Andrew would make a better
partner but put forward my personal view that husbands and
wives should try to stay together. I insisted that whatever she
decided, my help would still be available. Not least, I urged
her to be honest with George.

Mrs Weaver was no coward. She refused to write to George
to break the news but asked if I would take her. Anne and
Bet came along and she asked if I would stay initially in case
George was violent. I couldn't understand why people had this
belief that I could stop violence. George could have hammered
me into the ground with his left hand. Perhaps the idea was
that in the 30 seconds it took to hammer me the other victim

could run away. Anyway, I agreed. We met in the fish shop again. George must have sensed something was coming. We all fiddled with the salt and vinegar bottles. Mrs Weaver was about to start when the waitress snapped that we couldn't just have tea as the cafe was getting full. I groaned — did Freud ever conduct interviews like this? — and ordered chips. Mrs Weaver then broke the news. She was white and tense as she forced herself to say that she did not love George, that the marriage had always been unhappy and that she had found someone else. Anne didn't improve the atmosphere when she blurted out that Uncle Andrew had been in daddy's bed. George's reaction was to insist that she did not love Andrew, that she must give him up, that he (George) would change and be a good husband. I left after three-quarters of an hour taking Anne and Bet with me. My wife was going to meet Willie and Dolly but no neighbour would now look after Anne and Bet. As we drove back, Mrs Weaver said that George had threatened to beat her up unless she finished with Andrew but that she was glad she had told him.

Andrew now moved in. The fair season ended and George returned home. The bizarre situation was that Andrew, George and Mrs Weaver were all staying in the same house. I dare not ask about the sleeping arrangements. Andrew and George were either glaring at or avoiding each other but both refused to leave. George had a strong card to play — he was the father of Anne and Bet. He began to take Anne out for long periods, hinting that he would keep her. Mrs Weaver came to me in tears saying she would live with George if it was the only way to keep the children. Meanwhile, Andrew and George were coming to see me separately to say how terrible the other chap was and that they couldn't see what Mrs Weaver saw in him. I talked with Andrew about his intentions — feeling rather like a Victorian father asking if a suitor's intentions were honourable. I did not want Mrs Weaver to be hurt if Andrew suddenly made off, having had his bit of fun. With George, I acknowledged how hurt and humiliated he must feel. Mrs Weaver was insisting that she was in love with Andrew and gradually George accepted this. He was asking me about lodgings.

After ten days, I heard a commotion outside my house late

one night. Mrs Weaver, George and Andrew were quarrelling with each other. Eventually, George stormed down the road. Mrs Weaver ran in to me very agitated because George was threatening to throw himself in the canal. Andrew was calling after him to come back. A strange turn of events. Mrs Weaver wanted me to drive around the canal bank to stop the final plunge. I declined. My assessment was that George was getting in his parting shots. At her insistence, I phoned the police to let them know what had happened.

George did not try to move back in. He went into digs and only very occasionally came to see the children. For the next month or two, Mrs Weaver still wanted regular contact with me. She did feel very guilty about her behaviour, wanted to justify it and also asked me to find out if George was alright. She was wounded by the local reactions but gradually neighbours began to accept the change. Mrs Weaver decided that as she was changing her man she might just as well tell Willie and Dolly that George wasn't their dad anyway. I spent time with them, especially with Willie, talking this over.

For a year, I had counselled Mrs Weaver or the children almost every other day. Now, as Andrew settled in they needed much less help of this kind. Occasional crises did occur. Once, after a row, Andrew walked out with all the money. He was back within a day. He had been a young, single man and he coped remarkably well with the four children. Eventually, Mrs Weaver obtained a divorce and married Andrew. A baby was born soon after. And then another.

Finance remained a problem. Rent arrears had built up under George but he refused to accept any responsibility. Andrew was mostly in work but supporting a wife, six young children and back payment on the rent stretched them to the limits. They thus became regular callers at my house to borrow. Willie and Dolly would take it in turns to knock, starting with, 'Mummy says can you let her have . . .'. 'Mummy says' became a catchphrase in our house and was almost the title of this book. The required item was £2, the hoover, a toilet roll, a pan, an iron, panadol or whatever. To their credit they always paid back. At times, they were living from hand to mouth, borrowing because they had no money and six hungry mouths to feed. The project also managed to provide a few clothes and holidays for three of the children.

The older children became members of the clubs. In particular, Willie became close to us as he played in the football team, attended the Jucos club and often came round the house. Then Anne, now five, fell seriously ill. For weeks she was in and out of hospital. She had an unusual muscular illness which was likely to become progressively worse. She lost the use of her legs. During one long stay in hospital, Mrs Weaver insisted on being with her every day. We frequently gave her lifts and also regularly visited Anne. Neighbours played their part in baby-sitting. The doctors reported 'no hope' and Anne came home in a wheelchair. Miraculously, she began to improve. Now she is walking again.

Anne's illness brought in the local authority social worker to assist the Weavers. With eight persons in a small house they needed re-housing, particuarly as Anne could not manage stairs. At the end of the first three years, it is obvious that financial problems are going to loom large. But the family has held together through many plights and have established a foundation of family caring.

THE PROJECT AND THE PARENTS

The preceding four examples perhaps were not typical of our work with parents. They contained traumas and issues over which definite and clear-cut decisions had to be made. With other parents, I often failed to clarify objectives and sometimes must have left them feeling confused as to whether my visit was to talk about, say, the play project or the behaviour of their children. Our work with parents left much to be desired. Possibly Dave and I found it easier with teenagers because there was frequently a clear target — the reduction of thieving or truancy — which we could identify and work towards. Again, those meetings we did organize for adults centred around arranging activities rather than dealing with problems of child care, of marriage, of family relationships (although this has changed since Jane Thomas has joined the project).

The essential features of the project — being confined to

one community and providing clubs for large numbers of youngsters as well as helping those with specific problems — could be a source of difficulty. Parents might be confused about the project's objectives and sometimes we could be sidetracked from a personal problem into talking more vaguely about the clubs. On the other hand, these same features, what might be called the very nature of the project, could give rise to more positive spin-offs in the following directions.

Giving and Receiving

Living in the community, seeing the same people the whole year round, meeting them in good times as well as bad meant that a reservoir of local knowledge was accummulated which could be used in the times of crisis. Once I returned home to find a young woman, in tears, being comforted by my wife. She had argued with her husband who had given her a thump, walked out and not returned for some days. It happened that I knew where he was, indeed I had been talking with him about his marriage just a couple of hours before. The wife was frantic to know what was happening but scared of being hit again. I popped back to see him and they met for a long discussion. There was no happy ending, they agreed to split up. But, at least, they did reach a decision and she was not left in more suspense. Again, a mother arrived in tears having been reported to the NSPCC for child neglect. The inspector followed. Having known the family for two years, I confirmed that the clothing of the children and the state of the home could create the impression of neglect but that the emotional care of the children was very good. More frequently, the knowledge was useful in determining when a crisis was not a crisis. A woman might come crying that her marriage was ended and that she was clearing off. Our anxiety and need to do something quickly could be modified by the knowledge that the woman tended to act dramatically when emotionally upset and that the action required was for us to sit tight and listen to her.

Most important, living with a community, knowing people as neighbours, as fellow shoppers, as parents whose children attend the same school, means that residents can be seen as people who give as well as receive. We believe that the capacity to give, to contribute, is an essential part of human behaviour. People who become just the recipients of other people's help or charity may feel degraded or less than human. Perhaps one of the major weaknesses of modern social work is that it is predominantly a matter of 'doing unto others'. The clients' reactions to being cast exclusively as an object of help may explain why they sometimes react with resentment, lack of gratitude or apathy. A subsequent chapter will mention how some residents were involved in the project's activities. At this juncture, I want to stress how the project's workers were well placed to observe residents as givers as well as receivers.

Consider Mrs Dean. An intelligent woman with a large family, she found herself in severe financial trouble. She had become gripped by gambling, a fact she wished to hide from her husband who was in poor health. Finally, she turned to us for help. She was distressed at having to reveal her problem but comforted by the fact that I knew her in another light. She took a keen interest in the welfare of others and indeed she referred a number of people to us. She never had to assume the role of just a recipient of aid.

Local people were also able to help us. A local dad mended the van. I was given plants, seeds and advice with my novice efforts in the garden. More seriously, people visited and took an interest in my son when he was ill. When Annette fell through the ceiling (we had a perpetual leak in the roof), injured herself and had to go to hospital, neighbours looked after my children and even brought me food. Help is more acceptable if it involves some form of exchange, that is, if it is not just a one-way process.

Practical Help
Everyday involvement gave rise to the receiving and giving of practical services – a lift in the car, moving some furniture, mending a lamp. Often these acts were seen as and accepted as no more than residents helping each other out. But occasionally they were something more. The taking of a handicapped girl to Sunday School made a break for a mum with a large family. When a local dad, who had often criticized us, overslept, he took up our offer of a lift to work. A small incident

but one which served to build up a relationship. A closer
bond with a family developed after a mum stopped us in the
street to ask if we could help with a job application form.

Range of Services
The project was unusual in offering both clubs and a more
individual service. Consequently, a range of services was available, often to the same family. Thus, with one family we were
helping the parents with a marital problem, incorporating
their teenage boy into the club and occasionally keeping an
eye on the younger children when the parents went out. With
a lonely, unsupported mum, who was complaining of being
'cooped up' in the house by a large family, we could not only
visit her but also simultaneously afford her some relief by
taking the children to the clubs. At times, I think, parents
were the more ready to share personal problems with us
because they had already got to know us through the clubs.
Further, coming to the project or receiving visits from us did
not necessarily mark out a person as having a problem as
might happen when approaching some other social work
agency. As tables 4 and 5 show 19.7 per cent of callers wanted
to talk about the clubs while 27 per cent of visits were made
to discuss holidays, clubs or parents' involvement in the play
scheme. The nature of the project thus tended to play down
those forces of stigmatization which might inhibit people
from seeking help.

The above features serve to distinguish the project from
the typical local authority Social Services Department. However, the work with parents served to show that it needed to
be run in conjunction with the statutory service. The project
did not have quick access to foster homes, to powers to remove
children or to the kind of financial resources that might sub-
stantially affect large rent arrears. The advantages stemming
from the nature of the project could work best in co-operation
with local authority social services.

5 The Community

'We've done something together'

'Community' is a word which has already cropped up in this book. What does it mean? An academic book drew upon 94 known definitions and then concluded there was not satisfactory definition.[18] However, the authors did concede that a community involves a number of people living in a small area which is the base for carrying out many of their activities. As far as we are concerned, there is a small locality called Edgetown and people living there are ready to identify with that name. The activities of this community were important to us for two main reasons. Firstly, if the community helped its needy members, then many family and other difficulties would be lessened. Secondly, it was unlikely that the project would prosper without local support and approval.

In this chapter, we shall ask whether the community does help itself. Next the project's attitude towards the community will be considered, followed by an account of how this community responded to the project. Finally, emphasis will be given to the involvement of local people in the working of the project.

A CARING COMMUNITY?

Communities are often criticized for lacking community spirit. Politicians sometimes assert that the Welfare State has made working people selfish so that they no longer care for neighbours like they did in the 'good old days'. Oddly enough, these critics are often affluent people whose sheltered experiences have meant they have had no direct contact with working-class life. If they had, they would probably find that kindliness and mutual aid as well as selfishness can be found on council estates. Certainly, they can in Edgetown.

Most marked is the help given to the elderly. The estate still contains a number of tenants, now in their 80s, who moved in during the 1920s and 1930s. Most vulnerable are those living alone. The area has no clubs or day centres for the elderly. The slopes and hills can make walking a problem, while there is no easy access to a park. The bus service is expensive and not always reliable and the town centre a long distance away. In these circumstances, neighbours have acted as a social service. One widower is almost housebound following a fall and a broken leg. He depends almost entirely on the lady next door whom, he says, is like a daughter. She shops for him and goes in every day. In conjunction with meals-on-wheels, her friendship allows him to stay in the community. Interestingly, the woman has had her own problems with a hyperactive child, but she still finds time to help others. Another frail pensioner also looks after her middle-aged, mentally handicapped son. Her neighbour regularly takes her shopping in his car and clips her hedges in the summer. Another widower in his late 80s is also visited regularly by two women. None the less, the days can still drag and he once sadly said to me, 'My problem is silence'.

The community keeps an eye on the elderly. To a certain extent it offers services to children. Reciprocal baby-sitting is arranged. One woman gave much of her time to caring for a neighbour's large family while the mother was making daily trips to hospital to see a sick daughter. Friendships between certain families mean that interest is taken in each others children. This is particularly marked amongt those families who are related to each other. At times, a spontaneous action reveals a kind heart. A couple, who had problems with their own children, were going to the pub on a summer evening when they saw a boy sitting on the pavement. Knowing that— as usual—there was no one in his home, they took him with them to stay in the children's room with their kids at the local. The only organized activity has been by two women who run a boys' junior football team on Sundays.

Not surprisingly, the neighbourly service to children has many limitations. Some families are reluctant to invite other youngsters in, either because of overcrowding or because money gets nicked. Certain children are considered too wild, too dangerous or too naughty and so excluded. A few families are unpopular because they 'do not fit in' or because they have taken help from others but never returned it. A number of teenagers are looked upon as threats to the area as a result of their unruly, noisy behaviour. Thus, some families and children are too difficult for neighbours to cope with. None the less, the community still offers much help and many services to its members. Indeed, estates like Edgetown could hardly function unless residents showed a degree of friendship and neighbourliness which, in our experience, is less in evidence amongst those very people who tend to criticize council house tenants.

THE PROJECT AND THE COMMUNITY

Edgetown is a community containing families with strong personalities and attitudes. Initially, it was clear that the project could not succeed in its objectives without the support of the community. But, in addition, we believed that too often social services were imposed on people without their involvement or consultation. Thus, we determined not only to ask residents' opinions about how to proceed but, as far as possible, to involve them in the practice.

As explained, in the first weeks of the project, I knocked on doors. When Dave Wiles joined the project, we repeated the exercise in order to seek and collect people's views. From 1978, we published an occasional newspaper in order to inform the community of what we were doing and to invite comments. A number of residents contributed to the columns. Not least, we attempted to respond positively to what local people requested us to do. All the youth clubs, the football teams, the holidays and the mothers' group started after residents approached us. To accede to these advances created no problem in the sense that they obviously fitted in with the objectives of keeping families together, helping delinquents and providing family amenities. Other requests did not fit. However, in some cases, we attempted to help in order to demonstrate our concern for the community. Three examples can be given.

Firstly, people sometimes approached us about the needs of the elderly. In turn, we undertook some visiting, occasionally took them shopping, saw them in hospital, delivered a few Christmas parcels and, in the summer, encouraged the youngsters to dig a few gardens.

Secondly, we were asked to deal with an old and troublesome man. Light-fingered and with an unsavoury reputation, he had loud arguments with his landlord. Unfortunately, these occurred late at night or in the early hours when the landlord refused him admittance. Eventually, he gave him notice and Liam would come to pour out his pitiful tale to me. I could see the landlord's point of view. Liam collected rubbish. He toured the dustbins and took his findings to his room. He rarely had a good word for anyone. Yet Liam had his needs. I persuaded Liam to place himself on the council housing list. Relationships with the landlord worsened and Liam would knock on my door at any time between midnight and 2.45 a.m. Eventually, the council gave him a flat in the city centre. I still occasionally call on him. Once he came up to visit me. I had left him some new vests for Christmas. Liam grumbled that he wanted pants. At my suggestion, he asked Marks and Spencers if he could exchange them. They refused—not surprisingly, he'd been wearing them for a few days.

Thirdly, local people began to ask us to act as peacemakers. One family threw a notice board into another's garden and a quarrel ensued. The same result occurred when one person's dog scratched a neighbour's car. A feud broke out over whose daughter had fleas. More seriously, a distressed man and his daughter knocked on the door while a crowd of chanting kids baited them outside. We endeavoured to smooth things over.

Of course, the project could never claim to reach all the people in Edgetown. Nor were those contacted all positively inclined towards it. Indeed, we were often accused of showing favouritism to certain children or families. But the practice of consultation and response to local requests, in combination with the community's approval of the youth clubs, meant that many viewed the project in a favourable light. This was evidenced in two directions. As mentioned, people began to refer more incidents. The shopkeeper leaned over the counter and told me of a girl who had taken an overdose. A mother expressed her concern about some truants. Similar referals indicated that residents were gaining some confidence in us. Further, they began to support our organized activities.

COMMUNITY SUPPORT

Ambling along the street during the first year of the project, I was surprised to meet a TV crew taking pictures of a small, muddy, bumpy piece of waste ground known as 'the field'. Located behind some of the council houses, it is reached by an alley and served as a minute playground. I followed the line of TV cameras and wondered if a body had been discovered or if a local father's metal detector had come across treasure instead of the usual rusty tins. A group of mothers had also gathered, arms across their chests, scowling at the TV men. 'They are going to close it,' they informed me. 'They' referred to the council, 'it' was the mud heap. Sure enough, the evening paper and the TV news reported that the field would be closed because of vandalism, bonfires and motorbike riding in it. A gate was to be erected and it would eventually be made into allotments. The mothers were angry partly because they had not been consulted, partly because the action took away the only play area. A father hastily organized a petition which was presented to the local councillors but to no avail. Local youngsters showed their feelings by promptly suspending the new gate from the nearest tree.

The action occurred in the winter. The mums pointed out that it was in the summer that their children most wanted the play area. 'Can't we get somewhere to play?' one of a crowd asked me in the street. I invited them to my home and about ten agreed to run a summer play scheme. That first year it was held on each Wednesday of the summer holidays. The 3-8-year-olds attended in the morning, the 9–14-year-olds in the afternoon. In subsequent years, the activities were concentrated into one week as by this time the summer was taken up with camps and organized holidays.

Dough-making, kids charging around on three-wheeled bikes, paper models little girls dressed up as brides, little boys demanding piggy-back rides, numerous cups of coffee, stopping kids climbing on the roof. The first year was chaotic, especially in the mornings. The afternoon session also had problems as youngsters competed for limited equipment. A running fight between two boys resulted in two of the largest black eyes ever seen. But the mums and kids voted it a great success. Someone suggested an outing as a finale and two hastily booked coaches bore 98 of us to the seaside.

The pattern of play schemes and outings was thus established. Over the next two years, the scheme was better planned and organized. The mums took over the morning sessions, leaving Dave and me to head up the afternoons. Each year saw an increase in the number of helpers and children. In 1979 over 120 children attended each day with 15 mums as regular helpers The outings so far blessed with fine weather, are always characterized by children being sick, women paddling with dresses tucked inside their pants, older kids seeking out amusement arcades and singing on the coaches back home. The play schemes are valuable in that youngsters have somewhere to go in the summer. But they will be remembered simply because everyone enjoyed them.

The first play scheme and outing was enthusiastically received. One resident wrote, 'I can think back and I never remember any type of group outing or a party for the whole street.' Further, this collective action sparked off ideas for further community activities. In some cases, the parents wanted us to do the organizing backed by their support. Thus, it became customary to hold a parents v. youngsters sporting event on some Bank Holidays. Men have an annual football and cricket match against the boys, while the women play rounders and football. When the weather was sunny, families came with their sandwiches, while one of the dads brought his hot-dog van. We hired the swimming pool for family swimming evenings. At Christmas, Christmas parties and discos were held with the mums providing the food and a well-built father acting as Santa Claus. The first year we were dismayed when the money being raised for the party was stolen from a box in my house. The parents were angry and a number of dads got busy with a raffle that eventually raised more cash than was lost.

In other instances, parents have organized independently. The memory of an enormous Jubilee street party still lingers. One Christmas, the parties were planned and prepared independently and we just attended. Last year, the mums ran jumble sales and raffles and contributed £54 to the play scheme and outings.

Of course, not all, not even most, parents actively supported these events. But a substantial number did and it was not without importance. The joint involvement meant that we got to know each others' strengths and weaknesses. The mums were able to observe the way we treated youngsters and to decide, for instance, whether they could trust us to take them away on holidays. Sometimes, the events were a means of contacting parents who would not otherwise have approached us. One father had been deserted by his wife and left with four young children. Neighbours began to nudge me, 'You ought to help him, Bob, do something about it.' But my attempts to converse made little headway as he appeared to see me as 'the welfare'. One summer his children came to the play scheme. He brought and fetched them and sometimes stayed to watch. He accompanied them on the outings and became accustomed to talking to us. The outcome was a relationship through which we were able to give some individual help.

The parental backing also gave rise to a greater sense of unity. Leaving the coach and walking up the street after the first outing, a mother said to me, 'This is the first time we've done something together.' That word *together* stuck in my mind. Perhaps the play schemes, the outings, the parties, the jumble sales, the Bank Holiday events, did increase the sense of caring for each other, a kind of valued togetherness. This may sound sloppy and soft. Far from it, when it embraced care for troublesome kids and deviant families. The activities have encountered some wild youngsters, yet the helpers never insisted on kicking them out.

Not least, the enjoyment of the organized events may even be carried back home. Dave Wiles, in his initial months on the project commented:

> It is good not just to take their [the parents] kids because that isn't the answer to the problem to just take their kids and do something with them and let them enjoy themselves. The answer is to get the whole family to enjoy themselves and be involved . . . They might take it back into the house with them . . . .

INVOLVEMENT OF YOUNGSTERS

Parents were not the only ones who lent a hand. Mention has been made already of senior youth club members who participated in the running of the clubs. In addition, we encouraged older youngsters to accept responsibility for helping at junior clubs. At the time of writing, the Junior Club on a Monday has seven to eight helpers. One teenage girl is particularly adept at stimulating craft work and has the capacity—not always evident amongst the helpers—of sticking at the same task for the whole evening. Two boys run the cafe and man the record player. Another ensures that the table tennis is not hogged by the same players all evening. Following some serious violence at school, one boy was punished by his parents by having to be in early at nights. Unable, therefore, to attend Senior Club, he asked if he could assist at Junior Club, where he proved a capable and reliable helper. Again on Tuesdays, a couple of 16-year-olds will attend to referee and officiate at the boys' club. Enthusiasm was also in evidence at the summer play scheme where a handful of teenage girls were prepared to spend time with the little children. At times, we have had a quiet chuckle to ourselves at the sight of hulking male teenagers prancing around with small kids on their backs. Not least, these helpers were prepared to lift, sweep and clean. All our clubs are in hired halls and the equipment has to be put out and put away each time. Occasionally, we arrived behind schedule due to other commitments and, with relief, saw that the teenagers had completed all the heavy work. In the winter, our practice was to drive all small children back to their streets. By the time we returned the hall was cleared and swept.

Helpers were not all angels of light. Some could hinder rather than help. At times, a task was completed more slowly and less efficiently than if an adult undertook it. A 15-year-old girl came to help the junior girls at swimming. She caused an uproar by releasing the catch on the sunshade/umbrella at our table at the pool cafe. It enveloped several giggling girls and me. As I struggled unsuccessfully to escape, the manager arrived to inform me that if I could not control the youngsters then I should go. More seriously, a particular difficulty arose over a 16-year-old. An immature and disruptive lad, he came to help while unemployed. But his helping involved playing to win at all games. This was not too worrying at table football but it hurt when he boxed the juniors. Further, the club was trying to cope with an 11-year-old referred by the Child Guidance Clinic. The helper's means of coping was to belt him round the ear. Twice the 11-year-old ran out in tears and made his way home — once in pouring rain. Finally, I had to ask the teenager not to come. I had failed to help him or the club.

Generally, however, the involvement of youngsters had more positive outcomes. No doubt, for some, it served to fill in time. They enjoyed mixing with their friends and with the juniors. Now and again, they might learn something about themselves. I watched an older boy, often in trouble at school and with the law, continually reprimanding a troublesome junior. Finally, the latter swore violently, lost his temper and stormed off to promote more trouble. Afterwards we discussed the incident, when the helper was insisting that the offender be chucked out of the club. I reminded him of some of his escapades at school and Senior Club. The penny dropped. He smiled as he saw that he was criticizing the very behaviour which he often inflicted on others. I don't know if it affected his own reactions but he dropped the plea for expulsion.

In these, and other ways, we hope that a few teenagers are being equipped for the future. In years to come perhaps they will be running the clubs on their own. For the present, they have certainly made our task much easier.

LOCAL INVOLVEMENT

Helen
As explained, a number of parents actively supported the project's events while teenagers became helpers at clubs. Another stage witnessed local residents becoming involved not just in the occasional events, but also in the more day-to-day running of the project. A few adults sometimes turned up at clubs to give instruction on boxing or swimming, but the main regular helper has been Helen.

Helen lives a few doors from our house. Soon after the project started, she was deserted by her second husband. She was almost overwhelmed by the emotional trauma, by the difficulty of raising two young and demanding boys, and by the financial mess left by her spouse. She began to call regularly, sometimes every day, at our home. We helped her sort out the divorce, access by the husband and negotiations with social security. She also gained much support from a neighbour who introduced her to the local church. Gradually, the tension and high anxiety began to lessen. Helen participated in one of the summer play schemes and immediately displayed a knack for stimulating youngsters into craft activities. Subsequently, we invited her to be responsible for craft at the junior youth club. Surrounded by egg cartons, glue, beads, sticky paper and children, she proved a reliable and skilled worker. The project has gained much from Helen's involvement for she injected certain skills which we did not possess. Simultaneously, the involvement has meant something to her. She became better known to local children and she received satisfaction from doing a task so successfully.

Dave Wiles

Chapter 1 has already explained that Dave joined the project in 1977 after being chairman of the youth club. Now more can be said about his background and involvement.

Dave came from a large family and has spent his life on the Edgetown council estate. His teens were a turbulent time at school, home and work. He became involved in heavy drinking and drug taking. His crimes included stealing, fighting and motorbike offences. Eventually he was placed on probation. A succeeding chapter will explain how Dave straightened himself out. He was working as a labourer on a building site when I first met him and a mutual liking developed into a firm friendship. Dave took a great interest in the project once it started, while his involvement at the clubs revealed his capacities. At this time, he also undertook a part-time youth leader's course with the local youth office. A period of unemployment followed before Dave obtained another post as a shop assistant. Eventually, a trust provided the cash to employ Dave for two years. When that period was up, the Church of England Children's Society were prepared to take him on board as a permanent member of staff.

In retrospect, I am amazed how quickly Dave adapted to his new role. He took some teasing from his family and mates about being a social worker. His father said he ought to go out and 'get a pick and shovel and start work'. But he could always reply with a joke. His own home was very overcrowded and Dave also became worried about the increasing number of youngsters knocking on his family's door. So after a few months, he moved into our home. Of course, I was pleased to have someone else to answer the door.

Initially, it was anticipated that Dave would concentrate on youth club work. He was already involved in the Senior

Club and his presence meant that a start was made on the Junior Club. His activities at the youth clubs were by no means confined to organizing games. He soon developed relationships with individual boys. Dave's own comment recorded in February 1978 is revealing:

> In the beginning I saw it as a youth club that kids could go to. Now I see it not only as a youth club that's got the value of giving them something to do but I also see that within it I can supply something to a kid who needs something, maybe just a friendship or someone to listen to . . . . Adam might come to me and talk about family problems or about times when he has been tempted to nick things. Others might just come to me, for example they might want to do something in the summer holidays or they have got a need which they think I might help them with . . . .

From these beginnings, Dave began to see a number of boys outside the clubs. In addition, as explained, we were concerned about lads from one-parent families and Dave initiated the Wiley group.

His work was not only with individual boys. Three single men took up much of his time.

Peter was in his early 20s. His childhood was spent shuttling between foster homes, boarding institutions and children's homes. At the time, he was living with his married sister on the Edgetown estate. Peter's moods swung from zany excitement to sullen moodiness. One day he would appear in bright velvet trousers, yellow check jacket and leather gloves convinced that he was Edgetown's John Travolta. The next, he would be unshaven, unwashed and unhappy. His contrasting moods made it difficult for him to find employment and Dave spent time with him looking for jobs. Peter was also helped by a capable local authority social worker, but Dave was on hand to see him for long periods. Frequently, Dave would bring him to our house and Peter came to the youth club and the holidays. Dave also spent hours talking with him about religion, the occult and girls. Peter was possessed of a charm that made him likeable. At other times his unhappiness was expressed in a bitterness and viciousness that made him difficult to tolerate. Eventually, his sister and her husband flitted from the council house leaving behind unpaid bills and no forwarding address. Peter was only a lodger and received notice to quit. Dave accompanied him to flat agencies, social security, the Social Services Department and the Housing Department. Eventually he received a council flat in the city centre. From then on, Dave saw Peter less regularly but co-operated with the local authority social worker who now saw more of him.

Eric was a friend of Dave's before he joined the project. A physically handicapped young man, Eric lived alone in a flat. He did not need help of an emotional kind, but Dave used to spend hours conversing with him, doing the shopping, cleaning the flat and rescuing him when his three-wheeler broke down. Eric is a great talker. Sometimes, late at night, I have changed into my pyjamas as a hint that he should go home. Dave, by contrast, accepted the demands on his time with great cheerfulness. After years of unemployment, Eric started at the local Sheltered Workshop. Dave's mum agreed to make him sandwiches for lunch and Dave took these down every day. At the time of writing, Eric is applying for training as a social worker.

Roy also lived alone. In his 30s, isolated, an alcoholic with a long history of mental troubles, Roy was permanently out of work. He occasionally saw a local authority social worker but found in Dave a companion and friend. Within their relationship, Dave supported Roy in his efforts to cut down his drinking. Then, believe it or not, Roy won £1,000 on a lottery. At his request, Dave administered the money. They purchased goods for the flat while putting some aside for pleasure. Gradually, Dave began to cut down his control over the cash. Still Roy remained dependent, often phoning our home five or six times a day.

He also suffered periodic depressions and threatened suicide. Once he phoned to say he had taken an overdose. We rushed to his flat, obtained a key, and an ambulance took him to hospital. Dave still sees Roy regularly. One day a week they shop together and then Dave gives Roy the rest of the week's money. On Sundays, Roy goes along to church with Dave and is gradually getting to know more people.

From working in youth clubs and then with individuals, Dave moved on to helping families. We had wondered if people he had known from a boy would turn to him with their personal problems. They did. In the early months, parents would stop in the street to talk about their children. Then one mother asked him whether she could receive her social security separately from her co-habitee. From then on Dave's maturity and respect for keeping confidences meant that people, many years his senior, were prepared to discuss their personal affairs with him.

The employment of Dave brought many advantages to the project. They are gains which would probably accrue to any agency which employed local residents. Firstly, Dave already possessed tremendous *knowledge about the area* and its inhabitants. He had gone to the local schools, played on the same streets, caught the same buses, boozed in the same pubs. He was used to talking to neighbours. Even after he left home his mother was a source of information. As Dave put it, 'She is often talking to me about people in the street. She told me about a lady that was living on her own with two children and often left the children on their own. She often tells me things like that which is a help.'

Secondly, Dave could *communicate with local residents*. As one mum explained, 'He doesn't talk above us.' His background, his experiences as a delinquent, his own dislike of school, somehow put Dave on the same wavelength as many youngsters. Certainly there were some boys—such as Kent— with whom I could not get on but who took to Dave. This is not to say that he did not have to work at developing some relationships. With a few boys, Dave put time aside to take them to table tennis, to counsel alone, to take to school. Even so, his natural tongue and attitudes gave him a distinct advantage.

Thirdly, Dave won *respect*. As a local boy, he had straightened himself out, was handling club activities and was enduring the pressures of the job. This achievement was noted by residents who began to show their confidence in him. As Dave himself observed when talking about Edgetown:

> Outsiders I don't think they would be made to feel too welcome, social workers or people like that. I know for a fact that a lot of the lads don't have much respect for leaders of IT groups, probation

officers and social workers, and yet they do have respect for me, because maybe of what I've established over the years, which is useful.

To cite an example. A couple of many years standing in Edgetown were having trouble with their son's stealing. When the incidents blew up into rows, the family would seek out Dave. As he went to counsel people so much older than himself, I thought what a tribute it was to his maturity and local standing.

Fourthly, Dave's own experience demonstrated that *change was possible*. Frequently, youngsters displayed a mood of fatalism about the futility of school, the inevitability of trouble and the pointlessness of trying to change. The goals of 'O' levels, job success and satisfying lives, as painted by teachers or social workers or people like myself, might be dismissed as irrelevant and inapplicable. But Dave was someone from their streets, their school, their crimes, and he had changed for the better. Thus Dave brought many strengths to the project. And, it is worth noting, he did so without receiving any formal training.

To sum up. The project would have shrivelled up without the approval of the community. A number of parents were drawn into its activities while youngsters became involved in running the clubs. When, in late 1979, Jane Thomas started as the third full-time worker, she was able to initiate a club for the 3—8-year-olds, which immediately had mothers as regular helpers. All this occurred on an estate which an official once dismissed as a place where 'people won't do anthing to help themselves'. The opposite was true. We argue that such community involvement is a twofold necessity. We believe that local residents have the right to shape what goes on in their areas. Further, such involvement means that the activities are run more successfully. We believe that community involvement should be extended to include paying more residents to take more responsibilities for the project.

6 The Job

'Sorry to call so late but . . .'

People often ask us 'What do you do?' 'What's the job like?'
'How does it affect your family?' 'How do you cope?' The
purpose of this book is to describe a community child care
project. It follows that an account must be given of the pace
of the job, of the impact on our families, and of the pressures
it placed on us. If other agencies consider setting up similar
projects, then this chapter may well prepare them for what is
to come.

DAY BY DAY

'What do you do?' The figures collected over three years give
some idea of the number and range of activities (see tables 6
and 7).

The number of visits to and calls from local residents has
already been discussed. These are my figures over a three-year
period. In addition, Dave Wiles was also seeing people. Dave
joined the project in its second year while he was still living

Table 6
Activities with local residents in three-year period

No. of visits to residents	1572
No. of calls from residents	2002
No. of club activities	611
No. of days spent at camps and holidays	52
No. of times delivered notes	73
No. of times went door-knocking	36

Table 7
Activities involving other adults in three-year period

No. of committees, case conferences, etc. attended	117
No. of visits to negotiate for project	86
No. of interested callers to project	80
No. of speaking engagements	48
No. of visits to professionals to discuss individuals	45
No. of calls from professionals to discuss individuals	18

at home with his parents. During that second year he visited 368 youngsters and 298 adults and received visits from 22 youngsters and 8 adults.

The 611 club activities cover any organized events including youth clubs, the groups, outings and sporting events. Excluding the weeks we were away at camps, on club holidays, on personal holidays, at conferences, etc., the club activities numbered 4–5 a week. After Dave joined the project we usually both attended club activities.

Also in the neighbourhood, I went door-knocking 36 times and delivered notes 73 times. The former occurred mostly at the start of the project when I was introducing myself to people. The latter entailed giving out notices about meetings or events.

Sometimes we took youngsters away from the area and over the three years spent 52 days at camps and holidays.

The vast majority of activities were with local people. In addition, some time was spent with professionals who were not a part of the neighbourhood. Thus, in three years, I attended 117 committees and conferences. These included area social work meetings of the Church of England Children's Society, its research committees, meetings of a number of other voluntary societies of which I was a member and the local authority's Intermediate Treatment Panel. Eighty-six visits were made to 'negotiate' for the project, whether it was to obtain permission to use a hall or to raise money on its behalf. Over 80 calls (92 people) were made to the project by interested outsiders who wished to see what it was doing. As I also addressed 48 meetings, it ensued that about once a week for three years I was spending about half a day talking about the project.

Not least, time was spent with professionals—policemen, health visitors, social workers and teachers—discussing individuals about whom we were concerned. Forty-five times I visited them and on 18 occasions they came to our house.

The figures present an overall view of three years' activities. In order to give a more detailed impression of what happened day by day, I have selected one week from my diary. It can claim to be a typical week in that one crisis occurred and several clubs were held. The entries have been shortened to save space. Beside it, can be seen the entries from Dave's diary.

Bob

Monday

(a) Saw to post.
(b) Visited Mr Scott. He is anxious to know when his wife will take the children now that she has been granted custody.
(c) Set up junior club.
(d) Following urgent phone call visited Thelma. She had taken an overdose. Rushed her to hospital.
(e) Arranged care of Thelma's children.
(f) Senior youth club met at my house. Had a discussion on 'race', then played records. 30 present, be glad when we find a hall. Finished 11 p.m.

Tuesday

(a) Talked with Rev. Grant about using their hall.
(b) Collected Thelma from hospital. Took her to her GP. Sorted out a theft from her meter.

Dave

Monday

(a) Took Wynn to print Christmas cards for club.
(b) Visited Co-op to try to hire their hall. No.
(c) With 3 boys, helped Bob set up junior club.
(d) Ran junior club as Bob had to go to woman who took overdose.
(e) Senior club — discussion.
(f) Took 4 boys to chip shop before turning in. Al was very aggressive.

Tuesday

(a) Took Wynn to print cards.
(b) Went to Youth Dept's meeting for youth workers.
(c) Took cards round to members to sell.

Bob	Dave
(c) Dolly called to borrow	(d) Spent time with Wynn.
(d) Wynn called wanting some company.	(e) Took Adam to SSD.
	(f) Junior club (Jucos).
(e) Peter called to tell me he had obtained a washing-up job—his first job for two years.	(g) Took Don to hospital.
(f) Junior youth club (Jucos). Daniel violent. Don fell off climbing frame. Dave took him to hospital, nothing broken.	
(g) Wynn and Adam stayed for rest of evening. Finished 10.30 p.m.	

Wednesday

Bob	Dave
(a) Did post.	(a) Took Aston and Ant to visit Mick at Approved school.
(b) Wynn called and delivered notes for party.	
(c) Mrs Hurst called—financial problems.	(b) Visited school about Aston.
(d) Delivered food for Wynn's mum.	(c) Went to college.
(e) Arranged club outing.	(d) Went shopping for Eric.
(f) Wynn called and stayed.	(e) Took Conn to see his brother.
(g) Delivered notes re Wiley Group.	(f) Held committee of senior club.
(h) Visited Mr Peters who has offered to run a raffle for club funds.	
(i) Visited Mrs Field as she was lonely.	

Thursday

Bob	Dave
(a) Took Wynn to London. First time he has been on underground. Went to stay with Mr Laurie Laken, an	(a) Went to examine a mini-bus.
	(b) Helen called wanting to see Bob.

Bob	Dave
old friend of mine, who has got to know Wynn.	(c) Visited Mrs Long re her children.
(b) Went to Society's head-quarters.	(d) Met Mack in town—obviously truanting. Took him back to Bob's. Discussed his feelings about not having a dad.
(c) Spoke to London meeting on work of the project.	(e) Took Wiley Group. Good night. Daniel more co-operative.

Friday

Bob	Dave
(a) Returned home with Wynn. He had particularly enjoyed the trampoline training at Laurie's centre.	(a) Went to college.
	(b) Took food to Eric who is ill at home.
(b) Adoption visit to the Suttons.	(c) Spoke to Ant who is worried about his brother.
(c) Colin called re football.	(d) Wiley Group on special outing.
(d) Took Wiley Group on an outing.	(e) Committee at church re youth work.
(e) Visited Mr Peters re the raffle.	

Saturday

Bob	Dave
(a) Took junior boys for 5-a-side football competition.	(a) Football.
(b) John called. Caught by police doing break-in. Wants my help.	(b) Took Al and Wynn to work at salvage yard.
	(c) Visited Mrs Wells re helping at party.
(c) Adam called having heard about John.	(d) Visited Mrs Tasker re helping at party.
(d) Community policeman called. Is suspicious about some of the local boys.	(e) Helped at young people's club at church.
(e) Aston, Al and Wynn called. Cold and wanting something to do. Left at 10 p.m.	

Bob	Dave

Sunday

(a) Colin and Joe came for coffee and chat.

Day off.

(b) Monty, Reg and Tom called—bored.

(c) Adam, John and Maurice called to wash car.

(d) Wynn called for a chat.

(e) Took Mick back to community school. John, Wynn and Maurice came for the ride.

(f) Went to church. Wynn came.

(g) Aston came round for an hour.

(h) Adam called for a late coffee.

The figures and diary do not mention the many phone calls, the numerous conversations in the street, the discussions between Dave and myself. But they serve to give an impression both of our range of activities and our routine. It is worth asking how these compare with the work of local authority social workers. A recent piece of research, published by the government, *Social Services Teams: The Practitioner's View*[19] provides a detailed look at such workers some of whose caseloads were made up of families and children considered 'at risk'. Like us, the council social workers made visits and received calls, they attended meetings and liaised with other professionals. But some striking contrasts also emerged. Firstly, and obviously, they held statutory obligations which we, the project workers, did not. Secondly, we spent much of our time at club activities which were almost unknown to the local authority workers. It followed, thirdly, that we spent much more of our time with people who would not need to approach social work agencies. Fourthly, we had few administrative responsibilities. We endeavoured—and the Church of

England Children's Society was flexible enough to let us go our own way—to keep form-filling and record-keeping to a minimum. By contrast, administrative chores often weighed heavily on employees of the Social Services Department. No doubt these differences sprang from the contrast between a small voluntary project based on a home and working along-side a neighbourhood with large-scale statutory agencies often based so that their workers had to travel to where their clients lived.

IMPACT ON OUR FAMILIES

With the home as the centre and numerous knocks on the door, it is clear that the project must have impinged on the family and social life of Dave and myself.

The Home as a Market
At times, the home was like a busy market. While trying to write this very chapter, I jotted down what was happening. It was subsequent to the first three years and by this time Jane Thomas had joined us. But it typifies the rush about the house. 12 noon. Dave is making and taking phone calls. A pregnant girl calls to see Jane. Four boys drop in for a bowl of soup, a game of table tennis and a chat before we make sure they return to school. A lone mum comes to see me and stays to lunch. Soon after lunch, two unemployed teenagers call for help with getting jobs. A mother with her baby wants to speak privately with Jane so we find a space in the front room. Dave runs the pregnant girl home. My children arrive home from school and I prepare tea. Three times the knocker goes as boys ask about the club. Jane pops out to do a visit. Dave goes to meet his girlfriend. Jane is back in time for a regular session with a teenage girl. The two unemployeds leave. Colin, who helps at clubs, comes in. After a hurried meal, Dave, Colin and I leave for Junior Club at 6 p.m.

It will be realized that much of the individual contact with local residents occurred in our home. So did collective contact. The youth clubs sometimes met there, films were shown in what was once the waiting room, groups of boys almost always dropped in at lunchtime and Sunday tea time. Meetings with parents, committees, games evenings, etc. all took place in the home. In addition, the project's equipment, noticeably the club gear, was stored in the home, taken out and then brought back after the clubs. One result was quite considerable wear and tear on the fabric of the home. The carpet took on an attractive coffee-coloured hue encircled by a few cigarette burns. The railings on the stairs—where youngsters sit when crowded—tended to snap frequently. Despite our educative campaigns, regular customers still preferred to balance on two legs or a chair, to pick at anything pickable, and to place large Dr Martin boots on anything resembling wooden furniture.

My wife Annette cheerfully accepted all this. She also tolerated occasional break-ins, broken windows and very high gas and electricity bills. Sometimes she came home to find people in every downstairs room. What did get her goat was calls during meal times. We like to sit down as a family to one main meal a day but all too often it was disturbed by knocks on the door and phone calls. Sometimes, too, we ate as clubs took place in another room so that every now and then a boy popped in with 'a really urgent message' like 'Have you got a pack of cards?' Also she was not very pleased when a young visitor undid and threw a bottle of permanent blue ink over our best carpet. Annette says that her other main source of irritation has been to have project equipment constantly dumped all over the house.

The project could not have functioned without Annette's tolerance. But she gave backing as well as tolerance. She took an active interest in some of the youngsters, counselled people who arrived in distress while Dave and I were out, ran local mums to hospital, helped at the play project and jumble sales, gave lessons to backward youngsters and gave our footballers numerous lifts. Moreover, at times she decided I'd had enough and protected me. I've known her to leap out of bed at 2 a.m. and tell someone to 'clear off'. Thanks, Annette.

What of my children? My daughter Ruth, now 15, has always adopted a healthy cynicism towards social work and loved to poke gentle fun at Dave Wiles and me. She often endured great inconveniences, sometimes picking her way over bodies strewn on the floor as she made her way upstairs. Once her cello was broken by two lads playing around. Her chief complaints were that the house permanently stank of cigarette smoke and that her beloved guinea pigs were disturbed by the flow of callers. For all that, she cheerfully answered the phone and door, helped at the community activities and enjoyed attending the disco classes.

Ruth attends the local girls' comprehensive school but it is over a mile from our home. David, now 14, is at the boys' comprehensive which is on our doorstep. When the project commenced, Annette and I wondered if we were putting David at risk. In short, we worried that he might turn into a delinquent or truant. So far so good. He has mixed in, joined the clubs, played in the cricket and football teams. Occasionally, showing irritation at frequent knocks, he rushed to the door and demanded, 'Yes, what do you want now?' More often he tried to help. Once he found three small children sitting on their doorstep. He brought them to our house until mum who had been waiting three hours at the social security office —returned. David enjoyed having Dave Wiles live with us. In some ways, he saw Dave as a kind of hero figure. None the less, he had to share his home in a way not usual for lads of his age. Nearly every day, when he came in for lunch, David found other boys there. Never once has he grumbled. Thanks David. Without the backing and love of my family, I would have found it impossible to do this job.

The project, then, had considerable impact on my family and home. What of Dave Wiles? I have already said that initially Dave took a bit of stick about being a social worker. His family and mates would sometimes laughingly tell him 'to get his hands dirty'. But Dave's impression is that generally his parents felt proud of the work he was doing. His most serious worry concerned his teenage brother. Dave gave much time to other boys, including some whom his brother disliked. He sensed that the latter's aggression was partly a resentment about this practice. Dave tried to compensate by taking his brother out and paying more attention to him and to his other brother and sister.

After a year, Dave moved into our house and was followed by his girlfriend, Donna. The home was now full with Dave sleeping in the front room downstairs. Even so, it was still less crowded than his parents home. The move had two main advantages. Dave's parents were saved the knocks on their door while Dave could help answer our door! Yet there were times when Dave and Donna longed to be away on their own.

THE PRESSURES OF THE JOB

It would be false to deny that the project created severe pressures for us workers. We were often faced with people at the end of their tether, even threatening suicide. They brought problems, particularly about money or housing, which we were unable to solve. Then, at times, we felt shattered by disappointment, as when a boy, who seemed to be improving, stole from us. Dave had an old banger which was stolen and smashed beyond repair by a lad he had helped. His next vehicle, an old van, had the seats slashed and was finally ruined when some vandals set fire to it. Another pressure came from incidents which had no satisfactory solution. The huge flagpole outside one church hall came crashing down and smashed into pieces. Damage was done to a bike (not belonging to us) while using a school hall. The victims naturally wanted payment for the damage and punishment for the culprits. But no culprit could be traced. These pressures became intensified

by the strain of long hours. I recall one day which started at 7.45 a.m. with a boy having hurt himself, dealing with callers in the morning, receiving a phone call from a man saying he had just swallowed 40 valium tablets—just as we were starting lunch—looking after a teenager in the afternoon, having 60 youngsters and a couple of fights at Junior Club and a boister-ous Senior Club. The day finished at midnight with hardly a break. Such a day was not typical but frequently we did work late.

These pressures will be appreciated by many local authority social workers. They, too, are subjected to impossible demands, disappointments and long hours. No doubt they also experi-ence different pressures resulting from their obligation to carry out certain statutory duties. Dave and I, as project workers, also faced pressures not common to council social workers. For instance, there were pressures from both indivi-duals and clubs. Local authority social workers are used to the former but we also endured the sometimes exhausting difficulty of controlling large numbers. Further, having no premises, we faced the continuing worry of finding somewhere to meet. Returning home from a week's camp one weekend, I received a call to say we could not use the church hall as the decorators had not finished. The summer play project was due to start the next day! After hectic negotiations and the moving of the interior scaffolding until 11 p.m. we managed to proceed.

The main difference, and the major pressure, however, is that a home is never closed. It thus became extraordinarily difficult to take time off. I once tried to take a few days holi-day at home in the hope of catching up on some jobs in the house. In that period there were 41 knocks on the door (accompanied by 66 people) not to mention phone calls. A couple of urgent matters arose concerning suspected child neglect which also involved some visits. Even after returning from a week's holiday away, I found a boy waiting to discuss a court appearance. Within a few minutes of opening the door a man wanting some company appeared as did two other boys.

Similarly, evenings, weekends and Bank Holidays were rarely free. Often the evening call would start with 'Sorry to call so late but . . . '. And we were at work again. In the year 1978–79, I had only 95 free evenings. This did not mean that the other 270 evenings were filled with project events but rather that after 6 p.m. on those evenings I undertook at least one activity to do with the job. Of the 52 Saturdays there were only five and of 53 Sundays also only five in which nothing happened concerning the project. Thus I was separated from the job for few prolonged periods. Indeed, the line between work and non-work became almost impossible to distinguish.

Considering these pressures, it is not surprising that sometimes Dave and I hit lows, felt ill or were just exhausted. An old man I was visiting pointed to a grandfather clock and said 'That clock is over forty years old and never stops.' Often we were the same, all wound up and never stopping—I was also over forty. Dave was speaking for both of us when he once said:

> I think my decision to carry on with the project is a bit more fragile. A couple of times—that time when Wynn stretched me a bit and also when Ant has been fighting, then I have almost found myself thinking 'that's it, I can't carry on any more, I just can't cope with it' although I don't show that outside. May be I just get angry, that's the only thing I do show, but I sometimes feel I don't think I can manage any more and I wish I wasn't here.[20]

But somehow we survived and our commitment revived.

COPING

How did we survive? Mention has already been made of the support of my wife and children. Dave has told me how much Donna, his fiancee, (now his wife) meant to him when he was down. In addition, five other factors have been important. Firstly, we must be careful not to exaggerate the demands of the job. The long hours worked might include playing table tennis with a boy or even taking a group to a speedway match. Very enjoyable. Some of the knocks at the door were straightforward requests dealt with in a minute or two.

Secondly, we were upheld by local backing. The support of parents at the organized activities, the cheerful words in the streets, the offers of help. Their involvement meant that responsibilities could be shared.

Thirdly, the friendship between Dave and myself. We were more than colleagues. A caring for each other developed. As the older member I always felt a responsibility for Dave but he was just as protective towards me. In an interview, Dave was asked how he escaped the pressures. He replied, 'Bob, suggested that one night a week I go upstairs into the little room and he puts the TV on or a cassette in and locks me in. But he's just the same. I worry about him as much.'

When I was feeling pressure, Dave would act to relieve me. If ill, we would insist the other person took some time off. Occasionally, we differed about the way in which one of us handled a youngster or incident but the feeling of fellowship was never broken. This 'one-ness' in the work sustained us when things were going wrong.

Fourthly, the job brought many satisfactions. We enjoyed seeing kids enjoy themselves. We had a cricket match between Edgetown and the parish church. A ten-year-old boy came on to bowl at the vicar—no mean cricketer. The vicar took an enormous swipe at the slow bowl, missed and was out. My memory is of that delighted boy charging down the street afterwards, telling the world, 'I bowled the vicar out, I bowled him out.' Teenagers have called in to inform us that at last they have obtained a job. Younger ones have come to share the excitement of their holidays or outings. I recall two girls and a boy bringing their young sister round as she was recovering from a physical handicap and shouting, 'Look, Bob, she can walk.' And we have shared in christenings, weddings and parties. The enjoyment of others can be infectious.

Then humour has played a daily part. A woman approached me and asked, 'Do you know of any cub packs, clubs for nice boys? Don't get me wrong, I think you're doing a splendid job.' We saw a funny side to that.

Again, a group a youngsters were in the house discussing their lack of progress at school. A pregnant teenager urged them to do better than she had at school. As she aptly but inaccurately put it, 'Look at me, I can't read. In fact, I'm illegitimate.' The last Senior Club holiday was full of fun.

One evening Adam, at last, had persuaded a girl to accept his kisses. As they stood at the top of the stairs, someone crept up and began running their hands beneath his shirt. Adam, thinking it was the girl, began to respond with passion—until he noticed us. Jokes and quips have abounded. Our reply to the question, 'What qualifications do you need for your job?' has been sometimes, 'An 'O' level in corny jokes.' There's something in that.

Satisfaction also came when youngsters related to us. A lad knocked at the door and when asked why he'd called replied, 'Nothing special, I've just missed your company.' After Dave's car seats had been slashed, two boys—without being asked—obtained some needles and thread and sewed them up as best they could. A 12-year-old turned to me and stated, 'Bob, I'm definitely going to give up nicking.' A backward lad, who at club did little more than play darts with Dave, at last found the confidence to go swimming with the other members. Small incidents but important to them. Small incidents but important to us. They are the encouragements which balanced the pressures of the job and gave us the stimulus to go on.

Fifthly, both Dave and I have found encouragement and strength from our Christian faith. This subject will be raised in the next chapter.

7 The Church

'The church of what society?'

The Edgetown Project was administered by the Church of England Children's Society (CECS). As explained in Chapter 1, the charitable trusts financing the project considered it should fit into a larger organization. Within the city there were no voluntary child care bodies with full-time workers. The CECS had its area headquarters in the next town and agreed to sponsor the project.

'The church of what society?' people have sometimes said. Some still know it best under its old Victorian name 'Waifs and Strays'. In fact, the Church of England Children's Society is one of the largest national societies with a complex of social work teams, children's homes, day care centres and family centres. Initially, I feared that this very size might prove a disadvantage with our project being subject to excessive bureaucracy. On the contrary, such was the Society's commitment to preventive work that, while providing us with support, it allowed us to develop almost as an independent unit.

The Society is a Christian organization. Dave Wiles and I welcomed this connection for we are both Christians. We believe the Biblical teaching that God is concerned about social justice, social conditions and the quality of life in this world. Hence we regarded the purposes of the Edgetown Community Project as Christian. At the same time, we recognized that many non-Christians would also support the objectives of preventing receptions into care, helping delinquents and providing community facilities. So what difference did it make to the project that we were part of an agency which professed allegiance to Christianity and the Christian church?

In this chapter, attention will be directed at the use of church plant, the manner in which we explicitly expressed Christianity and the effect of Christianity on our lives.

USING CHURCH PLANT

When the project was faced with the demand for clubs and organized activities, an immediate problem became evident. The local authority had provided no community halls. One junior school was extremely co-operative and the young care-taker was a cheerful ally. The large comprehensive school had many fields, halls and gyms but, although individual teachers were friendly and co-operative, somehow the bureaucratic doors were hard, if not impossible, to push open.

Apart from the artist's pre-fab hut (mentioned in Chapter 1), the only other facilities were church halls. Edgetown contained four churches — methodist, catholic, evangelical and the parish church. Only the latter one had a minister. On the fringes of the district were two other churches. In order to use their halls, the confidence of officials had to be won. Some of the churches had already had experiences of starting youth clubs which had either petered out for lack of members, been unable to recruit leaders, or got so out of control that they had to be closed down. At this juncture, the title Church of England Children's Society became a positive aid. The churches were willing to listen to our pleas and after nego-tiations, usually opened their doors to us. At some stage, we regularly used all six church halls. They were rented for the clubs, the play projects, the film shows, the jumble sales, the parties, the Wiley Group and the parents' events.

Church halls did bring certain difficulties. Firstly, their committees naturally enough imposed conditions. We were always worried about scratching the floor, having the record player too loud, reving up motorbikes outside. Secondly, care-takers became all important. In one church, the caretaker backed us to the extent of covering up if we did anything wrong. In another, he complained if we left water in the kettle — 'it furs it up'. Thirdly, the halls were not always suit-able for our activities. Only one was large enough for indoor football but its leaded (and expensive) windows were so easily smashed that we rarely used it. Films were projected in one hall which was the right size for viewing *Dracula* or *Tom and Jerry* but far too small for anything else. Junior Club was held in the parish hall but the numbers made for frayed nerves. Craft work was situated in safety on the stage. In one corner was the TV game always in danger of collapsing from the pair boxing next to it. A piano divided the boxers from the mats reserved for fighting, with the girls' gym mats in the next corner. Elsewhere the painting group ducked to avoid the snooker cues while table tennis intermingled with darts. Board games, table football and subutteo clustered around the cafe. On a rainy day with too many kids inside and a few bad tempers, we were stretched to breaking point. Fortunately, the Senior Club met in a modern church hall, although somewhat too small for our needs.

Fourthly, the use of so many halls meant a nomadic life. We moved our gear into Junior Club as the play group closed down. Then at 7 p.m., as the whist drive arrived, we had to pack it all up and move down to Senior Club where members would be waiting outside — sometimes making so much noise that neighbours complained.

Notwithstanding these difficulties, the use of church property brought certain advantages. We became known to many church members who sometimes bent over backwards to help. When we could obtain the use of a film projector only on a Wednesday, one women's meeting vacated the hall to accommodate us. Further, the practice of using a number of bases meant that contact tended to be built up with different groups of children living close to each church. Possessing no property, the project was not tied to one place and did not face financial outgoings for structural repairs.

Generally, the churches made us welcome. They let us regularly use their premises at low or even no rents. Without their active co-operation, it is difficult to envisage how the club side of the project could ever have been developed.

WE ARE CHRISTIANS

The aim of the project was not to proclaim the Christian faith.

Yet Dave and I both believed that as our faith had made a difference to our lives, so our everyday living would inevitably reflect our Christian beliefs. Moreover, living in a neighbourhood where people saw us going to church and attending the chapel where many sent their kids to Sunday School, it would be impossible to hide our allegiance.

The question still remained, to what extent should we run organizations, formally connected to a church, with an explicit Christian content? Even before the project started, I had been involved in a club for 10–13-year-old boys known as Jucos. Jucos is part of a national Christian boys movement whose local branches are attached to churches. We decided to continue this club with its Christian emphasis. Its weekly activities consisted of: a meeting on Sunday mornings where we held bible quizzes, a serial, and a talk; a Tuesday club night; and often some sporting activity on Saturday morning. Jucos was the only regular club which contained open Christian teaching. Even so, we did not want youngsters to think that Christian allegiance was a condition of benefitting from the project. Thus, Monday Club was another junior club which had no religious content.

In Jucos, Dave and I had the opportunity to declare Christian values. After a nasty outbreak of fighting and victimization, I remember Dave giving a five-minute talk on Christian attitudes to violence. We also gave attention to our reactions to the elderly and the handicapped. As Christians, we were prepared to talk about the treatment of black people. One boy, Trev, reprimanded Daniel when he kept taunting one Juco as 'nigger'. Just afterwards, in the car, Trev was telling me how wrong it was to take the micky out of people because they were born black. Just then he saw a local boy and, sticking his head out of the window, shouted 'Oi big ears, they're going to use your head as the FA cup.' Obviously, our teaching still had a long way to go.

Christianity is not just about responses to social situations, we believe it also involves faith in Jesus Christ, the Son of God. Hence Dave and I were ready to tell members about our beliefs, about how we became Christians and what difference it made to us. We hoped that they too would place their faith in the same Christ for that is the meaning of being a Christian.

Sometimes the teaching couldn't have got through. I recall a boy telling me that he was trying to be a Christian because 'when I fall over I don't say I fell on my ass, I say I fell on my bum.' Others did develop a faith and were prepared to use it as a means of overcoming their problems. At times, I have been moved to hear boys saying they were praying hard to be able to stop nicking. Dave and I believe that God wants people to believe in Him and then to express Christianity in their daily living.

Jucos was the sole Christian club. Occasionally we held a Christian film at our house. In addition, our faith would enter our conversations. Sometimes youngsters approached us directly to ask what we thought about the Bible or what was the Christian view on marriage, war or abortion. Some of the youngsters once indulged in spiritualist experiments and one frightened teenager came to seek help from Dave. I also recall Dave being surrounded by a group of girls soon after he became engaged to Donna. 'Come on, Dave,' they were saying, 'do you sleep with Donna?' Being interested, I listened and heard Dave say that he did not and heard him explain his Christian understanding of sex, love and relationships.

On Sunday evenings, we usually attended a small chapel in a village about a mile and a half from Edgetown. It was run by one of our best friends, John, a long-time resident of Edgetown. John owned a small salvage firm and was a down-to-earth, practical man. His straightforward approach was reflected in the services. He never wrote anything down, spoke in earthy language and tolerated the noise of youngsters. He was a very humble man. He once said 'I'm even beneath the dustman. I take the stuff he won't.' Consequently, adults and youngsters — who felt uncomfortable in more formal churches where people wore ties and used long words — felt at home there. Dave was usually accompanied by Roy at the chapel. Youngsters knew we went and, if they wanted to go, would drop into my house for a cup of tea before coming with us.

THE EFFECTS OF CHRISTIANITY

What effect did Christianity have on the participants in the project? As far as I know many, if not most, residents on the estate contacted the church only at births, marriages and funerals. A number thought 'it a good thing' to send their children to Sunday School. Special occasions at churches usually brought a fair turnout. Only a minority were regular church-goers.

But church-going is not Christianity. We have heard some boys praying for help to overcome problems in their lives. Peter, Eric and Roy obviously gained strength and comfort from their beliefs. However, it is difficult to assess the effects of Christianity on individuals and here it must suffice to mention three people whom I do know well, Helen, Dave and myself.

Helen

As explained, Helen began calling at our home after her second marriage broke up, when her self-confidence was shattered and she was meeting difficulties in coping with her two boys. I also mentioned that simultaneously Helen was befriended by a neighbour, Fay. Fay called regularly and helped with the children. She was one of those beaming, modest and happy Christians whose quiet helpfulness made an impact on Helen. She began to accompany Fay to church and to a small Bible study group. Eventually, Helen too became a Christian. She talked openly of her experiences which also served to create a bond between her, Dave and myself.

It would be nice to say that Helen's conversion solved all her problems. It did not. She continued to meet difficulties with her divorce, in coping financially and looking after her children. On the other hand, she would say that Christianity became the mainstay of her life. Probably the most important gain was that this anxious woman learnt to trust God and thus became more relaxed. As well as identifying with the project, she became a Sunday School teacher and then its over-all leader. Sometimes she paused to wonder that a twice-divorced woman, previously an atheist, should be in this position. Christianity made a profound effect on Helen. I refer not only to her readiness to be less anxious but to the way in which she tried to apply Christian thought to marriage, child care and local problems.

Dave

Dave is convinced that but for Christianity he would not be associated with the project at all. Alienated from school, Dave drifted from job to job in his teens. Into thieving, heavy drinking and violence he was placed on probation. Worse, he was on drugs, soft and hard. Then Dave was invited to a Christian crusade in the city centre. Initially he rejected the idea with 'Crusade, I'm not Richard the Lionheart'. Later, when walking past the building, he decided to go in. He became convinced that God was talking directly to him. He walked out a Christian. A few days previously, Dave had burgalled an old lady's house. The depth of his experience was revealed when he now broke in again – to replace the loot.

Dave and I met soon after. We took to each other and a close friendship developed. Since his conversion not only did he change his mode of life, but he developed a much greater concern for those around him and, once the project started, he regularly helped out and then became a full-time colleague. No doubt, our similar faith cemented our friendship. At times we have started the day by praying together for the people of Edgetown.

Dave's conversion did not go unnoticed. He did not withdraw himself but even now drinks in the same pubs and mixes with the same friends to whom he made no secret of his new faith. Of course, he met his share of scorn and derision but also some grudging admiration. Older boys still tell tales of what Dave used to be like in his 'bad days'. He is an example that people can change their behaviour.

Five years since he walked into that Crusade, Dave is still a Christian. He has a conviction that Christianity should be made relevant to working-class people just as Jesus Christ entered the world as a working man whose ministry gave priority to the ordinary folk around him. Dave asserts that the Christian message applies to people's spiritual needs to get right with God and to their social and material needs. But let Dave speak for himself. I have explained that Dave was regularly interviewed by a researcher, Ray Jones. In the final interview, Ray asked whether Dave's religious commitment influenced the nature of his work. He answered:

before I started this job I feel I tended to talk to people more about my Christianity and during the job I have been very careful because I don't want to influence people too much. I didn't want to push people into decisions and things like this. . . . Now, after two years, I feel that I would like to involve Christianity more than I have in the past but there's two levels of it. My faith has really been great in the two years, things have happened which have obviously been outside of my control. . . . I remember times when I have really been at the end of my tether and have prayed and felt a lot easier, which is may be a thing that happens to all Christians. I remember miracles happening. I remember once Renee had an epileptic fit in one of the youth clubs, I sort of got hold of her and held her tongue down so that she didn't swallow it and I remember praying over her that she would be cured and it did stop straight away and she used to get the fits every three weeks, but now she hasn't had one since and I feel that that was something that God did

Almost I feel as if God is saying to me that He wants to get more involved with the community. I know it's hard and I think that another thing that has changed about my Christianity is that now when I preach I tend to dwell a lot on social problems and the need for the church to be more involved with community work and more involved with the people they are living next to. They have tended, I feel, over the ages to get more and more introverted and more and more spiritually minded whereas I think that is not exactly what the Christian gospel is. There is a spiritual side to it and that probably is the most important but Jesus wasn't someone who was just spiritual he helped people a lot and I think that is a neglected area of Christian life. . . .

Bob

Long before the project started, Christianity was shaping the attitudes and practices I would bring to it. During the 1970s I began to give serious thought to the application of Christianity to social issues and to my own reactions. Four conclusions seemed important. First, I believed that God had created the earth for the benefit and enjoyment of all men and women. There was no justification for some people to enjoy affluence and privilege while others were deprived. Second, having a common source, all people are in a family relationship with each other. Tawney used the beautiful word 'fellowship' to describe the concern and solidarity which should exist between them.[21] Third, Christ gave priority to people in most need. While not ignoring the affluent, the intellectual, the professional, He chose to spend most of His time with ordinary folk. He delighted to mix with those rejected by others – the thief, the adulteress, the leper, the beggar, the mad. Fourth, Jesus Christ strongly upheld certain values but was accepting of people who broke them. Of course, Christianity was not the only influence on my life. My family background, my education and my political allegiances all contributed. But I consciously drew upon these Christian conclusions both while deciding what job to do and how it should be undertaken.

Like Dave, I believe in prayer and frequently turned to it once the project started. The health of a local girl deteriorated so rapidly that within weeks she was in a wheelchair in hospital. I was moved when her mum told me that the specialist had said 'I hope you believe in miracles – that's the only hope.' I began to pray for her – telling both child and mother what I was doing. The tide turned. She began to eat – having nearly faded away. I sat by her bed and prayed over her. She revived and today is home and walking. To be honest, prayers for other sick and handicapped persons were not answered in the same way. But somehow it did not dent my faith. For, again like Dave, I drew upon His help while I was in need. When I was going to face that violent criminal, I prayed – for I am not a brave person. When physically and emotionally exhausted, I tried to rest in Him and so found refreshment. And, at times, all I could do was to say, 'Lord I can do no more. I must leave the rest to you.' This faith is a simple one for I am no theologian. It did not make me a better worker or better person than others. But I do think it enabled me to cope a bit better than I would without such faith. All the experiences I have been through in these three years have done nothing to lessen my conviction that Christianity is true.

To sum up: what has been the relevance of Christianity to the project? Dave, Helen and a few others were motivated by Christianity to try to help their neighbours. This is not to say that Christianity is the sole motive for other people became involved with no such religious influence. Next, the Christian concern and tolerance of local churchgoers was evident in their opening their plant to our hard and sometimes damaging use. Helen, Peter and a few other residents found Christianity a force which enabled them to relieve anxiety or to counter delinquency. Are we saying that it is necessary to become a Christian to avoid crime? No. Some youngsters may well be diverted from delinquency by people who have no religious allegiance. None the less, I sometimes look into faces so evil, so destructive, that it seems that only a great force or power will ever change them.

Lastly, Dave and I believe that the Christ has stood by us and enabled us to survive. Other people could do the job without our beliefs. Indeed, Jane Thomas, who has recently joined the project, does not share our beliefs. Thus a balance has to be reached. Christians must not arrogantly claim that their social work is inevitably superior, yet they must not be ashamed to say in what ways their faith may strengthen their contribution.

8 Edgetown Voice

'A better place in which to live'

This book does not claim to be a piece of pure, academic research. Rather, it is a personal and subjective account. Consequently, there is a danger that I have exaggerated the extent of the project or given too rosy an interpretation of its effects. Further, my impressions of the project may not be those of other people.

Chapter 8 offers something of a corrective. Part I contains the results of a survey undertaken in Edgetown by a research student, Sandie Lewis. Mrs Lewis's university supervisor originally approached us for permission to do the study. It was agreed to make the results public whether favourable or not to the project.

A sample of 30 people were interviewed after being assured that their names would not be revealed to others. It took place at the end of 1979 by which time Jane Thomas had joined the team. The survey presents their views on the project. Mrs Lewis's study is published as she wrote it, with two exceptions. First, her introduction about the origins of the project is omitted. Second, her extensive appendices containing a discussion of the research methodology and the interview schedules she employed are not included because of lack of space. However, for those interested the appendices can be obtained from the present writer.

In Part II, some written contributions by Edgetown residents are set out. Hopefully, Part I provides a more objective view of the project while Part II conveys something of its activities as seen through local eyes.

I PERCEPTIONS OF A COMMUNITY CHILD CARE PROJECT

by Sandie Lewis

AIMS AND MEANS OF THE PROJECT WORKERS

The aims of the community project, and the way in which the workers go about achieving them, may be open to many different interpretations by those individuals who are not directly involved with it. It was decided to examine these differences in some detail.

Knowledge of Work
People's perceptions of the scheme, and the work being done, are highly dependant on how much they know about it. Among those who were relatively uninformed, there was a tendency to place a greater emphasis on 'keeping kids out of trouble' and 'keeping kids off the streets', but the opinions of those with more knowledge of the scheme went much deeper than this. An example of this depth of opinion is provided by the responses from the youngsters presented below, which portrays a more perceptive interpretation of the workers' roles than one might have expected.

Children and Young People
Question (to youngsters): 'What do you know of Bob, Dave and Jane's work?'
Answers:
    'They help keep kids out of trouble.'
    'Just that they help kids and that at Edgetown — they run clubs, football matches. I went on holiday with them.'
    'Helping the estate — clubs and that.'
    'Make the street happy, so you don't get bored or anything.'
    'And visit people.'
    'They've settled this place down, I think, now. Because Edgetown was a rough, not very nice place to live.'
    Here, the youngsters have identified that Bob, Dave and Jane are working to try and keep them out of trouble by curbing their boredom in arranging clubs, outings, holidays,

etc. But more than that, they pointed out that they are trying to 'make the street happy' and one respondent indicated that the place had settled down and was previously 'A rough and not very nice place to live.'

A further question put to the youngsters was: 'What do you think they [Bob, Dave and Jane] are trying to achieve?' Once more, the responses were revealing:

'Make it a better place.'

'The kids get into trouble if they've nowhere to go and nothing to do.'

'They're trying to prevent us doing silly things like stealing and that.'

'If it wasn't for Bob and Dave, quite a few of the kids around here wouldn't have been to some places.'

'Well, they're trying to achieve friendship with everybody and they're trying to help them over all their problems – to keep Edgetown alive, like.'

'And trying to make us become Christians.'

'Friendship and peace, that's all.'

As in replies to the previous question, the kids pointed to the fact that they got into trouble when they were bored – when there was 'nowhere to go and nothing to do'. They knew that the clubs and other activities alleviated the boredom, and thus part of the problem, but several youngsters indicated that they saw more to the aims of the scheme than this alone, saying that the workers were 'Trying to achieve friendship with *everybody*' (my emphasis) 'to keep Edgetown alive, like'. Others referred to the workers peaceful influence and one lad, in particular, was aware of Bob and Dave's Christianity (which will be referred to again, later). All these views point to the fact that the kids see the project as much more than a simple provision of 'youth clubs' and view Bob and Dave as much more than 'glorified youth leaders'; a doubt expressed by a religious minister.

Local Adults

The perceptions of those adult residents who knew a reasonable amount about the project (and who proved to be the majority of those interviewed) held similar views to the youngsters, in that they mentioned the same points of practical help. When it comes to their views on the aims of the scheme, it was suggested:

'They make a sense of well-being in the area.'

'They create a family unit, which quite a few of the kids haven't got, I don't think.'

'They're trying to keep children out of trouble – but they're trying to help everyone else as well.'

'I'm sure he [Bob] tries to bring over a Christian influence, to influence those children in the home, setting a good example so that eventually they'll turn absolutely the right way.'

Again, the aims of the scheme are seen much more in terms of community development than in simply 'keeping kids out of trouble', and as in the responses from the youngsters, the local adults see Bob and Dave as 'trying to help everyone else as well'.

Professional Adults[22]

As might be expected, the extent of knowledge of the project among those professionally having contact with it tended to lack the 'gut reaction' evident in the responses of some residents of Edgetown. Knowledge *between* classes of professional respondent tended to vary much more than between resident groupings. An example of this variance is the comment from the community policeman that, 'They run the youth club at Edgetown – that's pretty well all I do know', compared with the specialized knowledge of other groups such as teachers and social workers.

The subject of how the aims of the project are achieved forms a substantial part of the responses of professional adults. For example, one teacher said, 'Social agencies tend to be de-personalized. Bob and Dave tend to bypass red tape!' And both teachers interviewed pointed to the obvious way in which the 'caring' aspect of the work came over, not only to the other adults but to the children as well. One teacher noticed children, 'Who seem overwhelmed by the care shown.'

This coincides with the response of a resident, who said, 'It's caring, and knowing they care about you ... when you're on your own it's nice to know people care about you.'

Furthermore, a magistrate pointed out that, 'Bob's personal philosophy is to make the whole area a community.'

Most other professional adults also felt that the project was not just about helping the youngsters. For example the local reverend, 'They are trying . . . to provide community awareness of the concern that is needed to be shown to young people. They are aiming at integration into the community, of the youngsters.'

Almost all the professional adults talked at some stage during the interview of Bob's attempts to develop a community spirit and awareness. One respondent (a social worker) encompassed the views of the others in his reply. When asked what he thought Bob and Dave were trying to achieve at Edgetown he said, 'Well, I think Bob would say that he's trying to achieve a greater sense of community awareness in that community . . . an identity, particularly for individuals within that community who haven't got that sort of feeling about where they live.'

It appears that the majority of respondents, whether child or adult, resident or outside official, see the project and the workers as providing facilities, care and support for the kids, while at the same time attempting to make all residents aware of each others needs, and working together with them to make Edgetown a better place in which to live.

CONTACT MADE, HELP RECEIVED AND ACHIEVEMENTS OF THE PROJECT

As proved to be the case about knowledge and aims of the project, the type and extent of contact with the scheme, and the nature of any help received, varies considerably not only from respondent to respondent but in particular between categories of respondent, so that, for example, the type of contact experienced by a resident would be very different to that experienced by a magistrate.

Below are some of the main points of contact as referred to by the youngsters.

Children and Young People

Question: 'How much contact have you had with Bob, Dave and Jane? How and why did it come about?'

Answers:

'A lot — we go places with them (swimming, club, football).'

'We go near enough everywhere with them.'

'Not so much with Jane, as she hasn't been there long.'

'I go to Jucos, Monday Club — and we go special places together, like bird things and that . . .'.

'Not a great deal, but only with the club.'

'I've had a lot — I used to go to Jucos so I used to see Bob and Dave a lot — and I go to church on Sunday night.'

'I don't see much of Jane.'

'I had to go to court so they came down there . . . and I had social problems so I come down to see Bob and Dave in the club.'

As one can see, the youngsters' contact varies from attending various clubs and going on outings, to 'visits' to the local Magistrates' Court! Some kids even feel that they can talk freely to Bob or Dave about 'social problems' at the community youth club itself.

When it comes to questions about help received by the youngsters or anyone he/she knows — the responses, once again are many and varied:

'They helped — [one of the group's brother] when he was in trouble — he used to nick stuff, but Bob and Dave got him out of that, and he's got a decent job now.'

'They helped — over the road a lot, 'cause he usually misses school, but Bob and Dave take it in turns to go up and make sure he's gone to school.'

'He helps my Mum, 'cause my sister's in hospital and he gives her lifts up.'

'My parents are divorced and my Mum can't cope with my brother 'cause he's so big — he hit her sometimes. But he's alright now since Bob and Dave have helped him.'

And from Bob's son, '[They] let them come in the house, have a cup of tea — they know they can come here for a cup of tea and a talk with Dave or Bob.'

Most of the kids saw Bob and Dave as doing something

positive for them, particularly those who'd been in trouble. One lad said, 'Mostly they've tried to straighten me out and give me something to do instead of getting into trouble.' Another lad, who had not been in trouble with the law, said, 'They haven't helped me out of trouble — but they've helped me in other sorts of ways.' That same lad was referred to, by a teacher, as having gone to Bob for advice when completing a form for application to a college course.

Local Adults

The adult residents also felt they benefited from contact and help from the project workers. One lone mum on the estate (of which there are many) said she had had a lot of contact with Bob and Dave, though she had only just met Jane. She met them through her son when Bob came to take him to football. Bob helped her with some advice about money problems. She pointed out that they had also helped a boy in a wheelchair who lived on the estate, and that they had raised money to buy him a washing machine. She then said that, 'They're always willing to help you — not just once and then you see no more of them.'

Another resident, when asked about contact and whether or not any of the workers had helped her, said, 'A lot — when the marriage broke up I was always along there for advice . . . I used to have to go along to Bob — mostly for reassurance — to decipher a [solicitor's] letter, that I was in such a state, I couldn't work out what they meant.'

Here, responses point to the fact that people trust Bob with even the most personal of problems. They also indicate that they appreciate support in times of minor and major stresses.

Professional Adults

Obviously, contact between project workers and professional adults is of a different nature to that of residents in Edgetown. Responses show, however, that the contact maintained can and does prove beneficial to local people, and in many cases makes the work of both the project workers and the other professional adults much easier to carry out.

Teachers at the local boys' comprehensive school, in particular, pointed to the advantages of contact with the scheme. Bob has been a member of a number of 'Care Committees' which are held to discuss kids who are causing concern. He had, in turn, received visits from at least one teacher about local lads. Bob and Dave often visit the staff room for a chat, and one teacher emphasized the success of this contact when he said, 'Last year, Bob "saved" two kids who wouldn't have lasted at school without his help.'

There are obvious advantages in maintaining regular contact between officials and the youngsters. The community policeman is of particular relevance here. Regarding his contact with Edgetown, the policeman points out that he has never been involved with their organized activities, though he has 'popped into club a few times' though not 'in an offical capacity'. Of the local kids he says, 'Basically, they're alright . . . they're kids, and they'll cause trouble given the opportunity, but basically they're no different than anywhere else . . . and half the time it's bravado anyway that causes the trouble.'

From the kids' point of view there is no doubt that getting used to meeting the community policeman informally has considerably reduced tension between them. The kids (even those considered 'hard lads') affectionately refer to their local bobby as 'Chipmunk'. Here, one youth describes how a group of kids first met him, 'How we first got to know him was, last Bonfire Night (or the one before) he came up and started talking to us − we sat down with the copper, playing with a hedgehog − we got to know him like that. We thought he was a right comic.'

Changes in Edgetown
When asked about changes in Edgetown since the start of the project, two kids, who were interviewed together, replied:

   (a) 'Yeh − there's no more law around your necks − they used to come up here every night before Bob moved up here − they're not up here as much now.'
   (b) '[Chipmunk] comes up here every night.'
   (a) 'Well I ain't seen him!'

(b) 'He walks up about four and comes down about eleven.'

(a) 'Well I've never seen him and I've crawled home all hours of the morning!'

(b) 'Violence has gone down.'

(a) 'Crime's gone down as well — there used to be scraps everywhere.'

The policeman admits that his colleagues may not feel as optimistic about Edgetown kids as he does — but can not wholly blame them as the kids' bravado often creates a false impression. He feels that prolonged contact (impossible because of pressure of work) would prove to other policemen that the kids 'are alright'. He feels that the incidence of delinquency is a little less that it has been, and that at the time of interviewing crime was almost non-existent in the area. His conclusion was that if he could spend five days a week in Edgetown visiting schools and clubs, and Bob could provide club facilities seven nights a week, delinquency would be alleviated altogether!

The youngsters also point to the fact that there is less fighting in the area (and fewer 'cops' about!). One social worker reiterated this when he pointed to the fact that Bob and Dave had 'stopped a lot of trouble'. The workers' effect on vandalism was noted by respondents on many occasions and the local councillor felt that if Bob left Edgetown trouble would increase again.

Throughout the interviews, in response to questions about contact, help and acheivements, a recurrent theme is the recognition, by all parties, for the need to understand one anothers' problems. The magistrate made a similar plea when he remarked that he would like to see Bob speak to the whole bench of JP's, 'As I feel that many magistrates do not understand youngsters.'

Some responses regarding changes in Edgetown since the community work project began have already been noted elsewhere, but additional feedback is noted here, accompanied in many instances by suggestions for the scheme and recommendations for the future.

One point that cropped up regularly was the uncertainty of many that enough was being done for the girls of Edgetown. The following quotation from a local girl may allay those fears, 'The girls used to get left out a bit — but then Jane came and that's all stopped now — we go places too. Jane doesn't ignore the boys, but has more to do with the girls.'

Even the local lads were concerned that there was no one to arrange swimming and other activities for the girls! One lad was pleased by Jane's arrival because, 'See, the girls needed someone really.'

There were numerous responses referring to the overall changes in the area; some were funny, some sad, but all, notably, were positive. Below is a selection:

You didn't used to be able to leave your clothes on the washing line overnight — or else they'd be gone the next morning. Someone took a jumper from our line one night — that doesn't happen anymore.

(local girl)

I locked myself out the other day and one of the lads got a ladder and got in through the window to let me in. That wouldn't have happened before.

(adult resident)

Yes, lots of things. It was all boring before. There used to be street fights every so often. But when Bob and Dave came it was all brightened up — there's clubs to take us off them things see.

(local lad)

Yeh — there's no more law around your necks!

(local youth)

You used to get the — Road lot fighting us lot down here, and us lot fighting [someone else]. I went down one time with a shovel! We still have our little feuds, but nothing comes of it no more.

(local lad)

There's not so much noise at nights.

(local lad)

Before, there was nothing to do all day . . . now you can come down here [to Bob's] [in the holidays] and ask for something to do the next day.

(local lad)

The kids, as always, had plenty to say when it came to making suggestions and recommendations for the future! Lots of them wanted to help with clubs, especially the toddlers club. Other suggestions included horse riding, more discos, shooting, adventure training, and, from one lad, 'Some things for club, to brighten it up.'

Another lad suggested people could help by, 'Just giving them comics and things like that, 'cause Bob buys all things like that and the games and that, and people just chuck things like that out.' or: 'We could make a sort of fund', suggested another lad.

Bob's son's suggestion for the future was that less people should knock at the door at meal times – perhaps because when asked about his part in the project, he said, 'I've helped run the clubs – and I answer the door every five minutes!'

Many suggestions and recommendations from the adults on the estate concerned the fact that local people should become more involved. As one local Mum said, 'I think you can always do with Mums.' Another suggestion from a local couple was for, 'More support for Bob from the Local Authority – buy our own Youth Centre. If the land was allocated there's enough people round here to build it – even sponsored walks, etc. could raise money.'

There can be no doubt that residents of all ages are conscious of the achievements of the project workers, while almost all of them have ideas and advice about possible extensions to the scheme. Bob, Dave and Jane all appear keen to hear about these ideas, and indicate that where possible they will try to implement them; certainly new activities such as parachuting and ice skating now seem very popular, as does the recently formed 'Mums and Youngsters' group. It may be encouraging for the workers to realize that the kids appreciate it when their views are taken seriously. As one youth put it, when asked if (and how) Bob, Dave and Jane differed from other social workers, 'They take different points of view, and they make it possible for each point of view to work. They listen to everybody first, before they do anything.'

Adult Professional Views
As one might expect, suggestions and recommendations from

the adult professional respondents were not concerned quite as exclusively with ideas for activities and the like, though many were concerned, as were the residents, about practical help. One teacher put it this way, 'I expect they [the project] always need money!' Both teachers tentatively suggested more 'ground workers' for the project. Doubts about the merit of this (where mentioned) revolved around the possible 'de-personalization' of the scheme, should extra staff in fact materialize.

A social worker suggested it may be possible for the workers to use ward councillors as a 'link' with outside bodies and agencies, if this could prove useful. The religious minister advocated more involvement with other existing local groups — such as young wives, church groups, etc. But the main suggestion which came from residents as well as most of the professional adults, was what was identified as a desperate need for some kind of community centre in the area (which as we have seen, the residents are apparently willing to build for themselves)! The local councillor pointed out, 'It's dreadful that there is no community centre on the estate.'

The clubs run by the workers make use of church hall facilities, as well as Bob's own home. At least one of the halls is some way from the estate. Transporting materials needed for the club each week takes quite a time, and involves lifting many heavy items. As the religious minister pointed out, 'There are a terrific number of youngsters not catered for on a regular basis. They therefore need a community centre and somewhere to go every night, not just once or twice a week.'

In fact, the local councillor informed me that there was a budget for a playing field on rough ground at Edgetown, which should be completed during 1980. And, bearing in mind the lack of a community centre, one teacher suggested, 'The use of school facilities in the evenings would be great — but this is more — [County Council] I should think.'

Perhaps a social worker's comment, when asked, 'What else could be done?' would suffice to show the general theme of the interviews with many of the adult professional respondents:

I don't know whether very much more could be done than what

Bob is, in fact, doing. The fact of his being there and of his house acting as a focus for what goes on, of being around, and by using the local church groups, I guess he's doing about as much as is possible.'

PERCEPTIONS OF EDGETOWN, ISSUES AND THE WORKERS

The Area

We have seen, in the previous sections, some of the changes that people feel have come about in Edgetown (particuarly from the youngsters) since the start of the project in 1976. Whilst bearing this in mind, I include here some general comments of perceptions of the area from other categories of respondent.

A magistrate saw, 'Simply that Edgetown is a socially deprived area — [with] some pockets of fair affluence — but even these have domestic problems.' He also felt Edgetown to be a very difficult area in need of this type of project — though he pointed out early in the interview that he had never been to Edgetown.

A social worker and a religious minister were not so sure that the choice of Edgetown for the scheme was necessarily the best decision.

I could think of worse areas — e.g. one very near Edgetown is —. This is probably in greater need. Edgetown has problems, but has more sense of community. It also has areas of private housing.
(religious minister)

Edgetown's a very divided sort of area — there's the private bit and the council bit. . . . I think if I were starting a similar project I would have moved a little bit more towards — [same area as that mentioned by the religious minister] 'cause Edgetown has never struck me as being the most deprived.
(social worker)

The community policeman, however, pointed out:

If he was to move off that particular set-up, where would there be [for the kids] to go? . . . I think there's a gap and that's where a

lot of the problems arose before. It always stuck out that there is
nothing up there for the kids to do — and so they cause trouble.

The residents themselves, although exhibiting that they
are aware (and feel strongly about) what they see as a lack
of facilities, point also to what they consider to be the many
'positives' of Edgetown. One local couple said, 'Other areas
don't have the relationship in the community we have in
Edgetown!' Then, as shopkeepers on the estate, said, 'Our
shop is a centre — a meeting place — a social centre.'

Another resident said Edgetown had become a lot more
friendly since she had got to know the children (through Bob).
The following extract is revealing in this context, as it comes
from a lady who lives in the private sector of Edgetown. She
is speaking about some of the council house tenants nearby:

> I used to think they were very scruffy, very noisy, very common,
> and not quite my type. But once you get to know them, they're
> ever such nice people really — there's quite a lot underneath that
> you suddenly discover — and I think it's done them a world of
> good to have Dave actually come from round there, for a start.

Issues

Each of the adult professional respondents was asked a question relating to any issues/incidents which might arise or have
arisen out of their contact with Edgetown or its residents.
Those interviewed approached the question in different ways,
so their responses may be best looked at individually.

One teacher explained that many of the school staff were
concerned, at the start of the project, that difficulty might be
created if Bob was seen by the kids as a link with the school.
However, he went on to say that this had not proved to be a
problem, which he sees as a great compliment to Bob.

Another teacher wanted the link between the scheme and
the school improved. He felt that information about the needs
of local groups would be useful when introducing lads to
community work and experiences.

A JP felt that the main problem with youngsters, 'Is simply
getting them through to maturity.' He told of the 'excellent'
idea of Bob speaking about boys in trouble, if they went to

court, and quoted one case where, 'Some boys stole bikes —
the teacher gave evidence which was negative and critical.
Bob stood up in court — he was not condoning the boys'
actions but was positive about them.'

A local Labour Councillor said that he had, in the past,
been contacted mainly with complaints about lads causing
a nuisance near private garages or on motorbikes. The residents
from a local block of flats had also complained to him about
young couples 'courting' in the basement area. He pointed
out that he had not received as many complaints since Bob's
arrival.

The Reverend felt that the issues raised were not restricted
to Edgetown — with the possible exception of the need for a
community centre on the estate.

A difficulty, as far as the policeman was concerned, is, 'I
sometimes wonder, if the chips were down, where he [i.e.
Bob] would lean to . . . if he'd be too much on their side as
opposed to our side? But if he was on their side, I'd understand his motives.' When asked if this created any problems
in his relationship with Bob, he said, 'No — certainly not. If
I'd thought he was doing it for the wrong motives, then it
would.'

One social worker felt that it would be useful if the project
could be used as a resource for helping different client groups
as well as youngsters. She continued by saying that Bob
explained, 'That he's not actually meant to go that far — that
really because he's being sponsored by the Church of England
Children's Society, he has to keep within certain boundaries.'

Another social worker, himself a resident of Edgetown,
said that people often suggested that residents should use the
facilities on other estates, but that he felt, 'Edgetown should
have something of their own.' He continued, 'There's very
little vandalism — though a lot of that's got to do with Bob —
and the kids are great there.'

Perceptions of the Workers

All residents, and those of the professional adults that had
had actual contact with them, were asked to describe the
project workers. Below is the profile that emerges for each of
the three workers.

Dave, as perceived by the boys and girls:
    'Good bloke.'
    'Good joker.'
    'Cheers you up.'
    'Ex-offender.'
    'A bit of a lad.'
    'Joins in with the kids.'
    'Can talk to him.'
    'More our age.'
    'Easy to get on with.'
    'Was worse than anyone before he turned into a Christian.'
    'Fits in right.'

Bob, as perceived by the boys and girls:
    'Bob's more serious than Dave.'
    'Good bloke — a laugh.'
    'Takes you places.'
    'Helpful.'
    'Generous.'
    'Bob's not all that young any more.'
    'Can go along with a joke.'
    'Kind.'
    'Peaceful.'
    'Takes a while to get round to doing things!'
    'He scares me a bit — he's got big hands!'

Jane, as perceived by the boys and girls:
    'She's nice.'
    'Nice lady.'
    'She doesn't try to act over us.'
    'Gorgeous.'
    'Very understanding.'
    'Active.'
    'She mixes well and is easy to get on with.'
    'Near enough our age.'
    'She accepts my help.'
    'Doesn't boss us about.'
    'Can take a joke.'
    'She joins in with things — like ice-skating.'
    'Jane understands.'

'Friendly.'

'We can give her our problems.'

'The girls needed someone really.'

'She likes playing table tennis – she beat me.'

'Our lot fancies her, I don't blame them – I'm one of them!'
The adults, not surprisingly, tended to view the workers in a
slightly different light!

Dave, as perceived by the adults:
Although Dave seems to be a very popular figure on the estate,
it is interesting to see that the adults I questioned referred to
him in quite a different way from the youngsters. Though
they, too, referred to him as 'approachable' and 'he joins in',
they also pointed to some aspects of his personality that were
not noted by the kids:

'Sometimes he talks very seriously about religion and the
Lord.' (local lady)

'I think Dave's a marvellous Christian.' (lone mum on estate)

'I think Dave's marvellous – he's a quieter type.' (female
resident)

'I've got most time for Dave, in the three, because he's had
a hard time.' (social worker)

'I've got a lot of time for Dave – for a young lad to do
that.' (social worker)

'Bob's sidekick as it were . . . much more the practical one,
on the ground, working with the kids.' (social worker)

Bob, as perceived by the adults:
Several of those interviewed referred to the success of the
project, and its dependency on the dedication and total
commitment of Bob. One of the social workers and a religious
minister, when asked if the scheme could be similarly used in
other areas, both emphasized that this was only possible if
that type of commitment could be ensured.

Below are some of the key aspects of his personality that
were referred to:

'Bob cares.' (resident)

'Realistic . . . not a do-gooder.' (teacher)

'Gives a father-figure to the kids.' (magistrate)

'Committed . . . helpful, enabling sort of person.' (social worker)

'What he doesn't know he'll always find out!' (resident)

'Is on hand 24 hours a day.' (teacher)

'Doesn't stand on the sidelines — joins in!' (shopkeeper)

'He's a first-class bloke and all his ideas are good.' (social worker)

'Got the kids' interests at heart.' (community policeman)

'He tries to bring over a Christian influence.' (resident)

Jane, as perceived by the adults:

Jane is the most recent addition to the 'team', having joined them in the autumn (though she accompanied a group of youngsters on a camping holiday prior to becoming a full-time worker). It seems, from some of the responses (see below), that Jane has established herself very quickly in the area. Most of the adult professionals had not yet met Jane, so below are the residents' views:

'I think she's very nice.'

'A lovely girl.'

'She always stops and talks.'

'She's ever so friendly — and such a tiny little thing too!'

'When I first heard they were going to have a lady social worker I thought Ugh! that doesn't appeal to me at all — I'll stick to Bob and Dave — I suppose I expected somebody old . . . but she's young, and the girls like her . . . I think she's smashing!'

It is apparent, particularly from the responses of residents, that the project workers are seen as part and parcel of the Edgetown community. The shopkeeper pointed out, 'The kids seem really to love Bob and Dave. It is understandable with Dave, with him coming from the area, but Bob's an outsider, yet he's definitely won their hearts, no doubt about it.'

AUTHOR'S PERCEPTIONS OF PROJECT

My contact with Edgetown and with the community workers lasted for approximately four months. Inevitably the extent of this contact varied, though it was never less than once weekly.

My initial knowledge of the work resulted from my 'briefing' by my supervisor, and Bob himself. However, it soon became apparent that there was far more involved in the scheme than I had at first supposed, for accounts about 'generally helping and advising' proved, in reality, to be somewhat of an understatement! It was not until I heard reports time and time again of Bob's 'open house' that I came to understand what people meant about 'commitment' and 'dedication'.

It would be unrealistic of me to suggest that I might offer an unbiased opinion of the success achieved at Edgetown. I do feel, however, that the views expressed by residents and officials on these issues are proof enough that the workers should feel a sense of achievement in the work they do. Several residents spoke to me, in confidence, once the tape-recorder had been switched off, of the difference that the scheme had made to their lives. One lady spoke of the loneliness she had felt in the past, but she had now become quite involved in helping with the project and felt she always had friends to turn to in Bob, Dave and Jane. More than this, she revealed that through the workers she had come to make friends within the community, who previously, as she put it, were 'ignored and ignoring'.

Many residents pointed to the fact that Bob was permanently 'on duty'. This certainly became apparent to me during the course of my visits to his house. In fact, it is a standing joke amongst the workers themselves. On one occasion when I remarked to Bob that I was surprised to see him at club as I thought he had expected to be at home writing, he replied, 'Well yes – in fact Jane's going to give me a day off next year, to write my book!'

Jane answered, 'Well I don't know about next year, maybe the year after. . . .'

From incidents like this, I tended at first to agree with respondents such as the teacher, who suggested that they could use more trained and paid helpers. But as time went on, I revised my ideas somewhat and now conclude (along with a different teacher) that although the workers always need additional help, an extension of the workforce could easily lead to the 'de-personalization' of the scheme. It will be remembered that the closeness of the project to the community was viewed by many of the respondents as one of the most important factors in its success.

I do agree, however, with the almost unanimous decision that there is an overwhelming need for some kind of community centre in the area. Using church hall facilities, although useful and very necessary at this stage, is not an ideal situation, especially when many other groups do the same. The goods and chattels of all the users are bundled together in a small storage room, and inevitably slight damage occurs. On one occasion, at Junior Club, a girl unwittingly sat against a ladder belonging to the playgroup climbing frame, which promptly snapped. Bob and the girl went to the playgroup leader's house to apologise. Fortunately, there was a handyman in the leader's family and the damage was easily repaired — but incidents such as this could be made less likely to happen by the provision of a proper community centre with adequate storage space. It may be heartening for the workers to note the following (from a religious minister), 'Vandalism or breakages were never a problem . . . they do no worse than any other youth group using the hall, such as Cubs, Scouts, Church Clubs, etc.'

Overall, I would like to say that my involvement with the scheme was a very happy time for me (albeit at times hard work!) and I found the people on the estate to be warm and friendly. There are several homes that I know will always make me welcome, should I visit the area again. I came to know several of the youngsters very well, and agree with the social worker, who said, 'The kids there are great.'

Finally, I would like to say that I have tremendous respect and admiration for Bob, Dave and Jane, and for the work they do — long may it continue!

II EDGETOWN WRITES

Occasionally, residents of Edgetown have made written contributions relevant to the project. These have been composed either for our project newspaper (which appears at regular intervals — like once a year) or were a response to our invitation to write in this book. The contributions have been grouped under four headings but they do not follow any obvious sequence. They are included simply because they present a local person's description of the project.

The Project

Bob bought a house on Edgetown estate and his job was a youth and community worker and he worked for the Church of England Children's Society.

At first Bob did not know how to approach the people in Edgetown. So he decided to start off by doing door-knocking. Most of the people were pleased to see that someone was at last doing something to try and stop the vandalism in Edgetown. Quite a lot of people said that the kids in Edgetown need somewhere to go at nights something like a youth club. So Bob spoke to kids in the street and they decided to have a meeting down at Bob's house about what they are going to do. So Bob had a meeting with a few of the kids and they decided to start up a youth club.

So we started the first Edgetown youth club at the studios but there was a bit of vandalism so we were asked to leave. Dave Wiles, who was about the first person in Edgetown to know Bob, became Bob's second man because Bob had raised enough money to have a second man in the team. After a while of Dave and I looking around for another place for our club we finally got our club going again at the church.

One day when Bob was sitting in his house he heard a knock at the door. It was some of the junior boys of Edgetown asking why

the senior boys of Edgetown had a youth club but the juniors didn't. So Bob, Dave and I started a Junior Club.

Both Edgetown senior and junior clubs are on a Monday night. Junior Club starts at 5 o'clock, and ends at 7 o'clock and then we go to Senior Club which starts at 7.30 and ends at 10.30.

We do another club which is more of a Christian club rather than a youth club. It meets on Sunday at 9.30 for its meeting on the Christian side of it, and it meets on a Tuesday for a games night. On Thursday we do a group called the Wiley (named after Dave Wiles) which starts at 4 o'clock and ends at 6 o'clock. And at that club there is about seven one-parent families and about eight two-parent families, and at it they play all kinds of games, and at the end have coffee and a discussion.

On Saturday morning the Jucos usually play football or go swimming. On Saturday afternoons Edgetown senior youth club play football.

In about the first week of the summer we help some of the mums with a play project so that the kids have something to do on the first week off school. And all through the summer Bob organizes day trips and takes the Jucos on a camp, and takes half of Wiley Group on one camp, and the other half to another camp. And Edgetown senior youth club go to Butlins for a week.

(Wynn)

At Edgetown, Bob Holman and his friend Dave Wiles, work together as youth workers and they help people to stay out of trouble.

I have been in trouble with the school for playing truant, but Dave and Bob got me out of trouble, not by lying, but by telling the truth and talking to me and helping me to understand.

A good example is a friend of mine. He was in trouble but now he swears, fights and argues, but he never steals or vandalizes things. But he still fits in with people and with the lads around Edgetown.

I am trying to go straight and Dave and Bob help me to understand right and wrong.

Wiley Group is a club which at the start of club we play table tennis, snooker, television game, etc., but at the end we sit down and we talk about serious things like stealing, truancy, vandalism, etc., but we do it in a friendly way.

Junior and Senior Club Bob and Dave run on Mondays. I used to go to Junior Club, but it was for 9 to 13-year olds and now I am allowed to go to Senior Club. I don't know why, but the club show they can handle us, but they don't push us around and tell us what to do. They ask us to do it, whatever it is, so we don't feel we are at Detention Centre or Assessment Centre.

Jucos is a club twice a week and it is for a religious sort of boy, but you don't have to be religious. They do quizzes and stories and club on a Tuesday where there is football, table tennis and snooker. With Bob and Dave you can ask for help and you get help.

Bob and Dave go to court with people, give them legal advice and they talk to the parents of the children who might have to go to court. I may have to go to court and I am going to ask for their advice because I have faith in Bob and Dave.

(Aston)

We arrived in Edgetown on a cold, wet, wintry March Saturday evening, 1979.

Everything was unloaded from a hired transit and jammed in our newly alloted council house.

We have four children, 3 boys, 16, 14, 11 and a girl 10. Life has dealt us many cards, some aces, some not.

The first week was a settling-in time where the children found new friends and we tried to get used to our new surroundings. The neighbours were (and still are) very helpful and friendly.

It was at the end of our first week when we heard about the Edgetown Community Project. Dave Wiles was first on the scene to make our acquaintance and we then realized we vaguely knew him from the shop where he used to work. He encouraged Charles and Gwynn, two of my boys, to join the Monday Club and Kate also joined later when she was old enough.

Gwynn, our 11-year-old son, joined the Juco Club run by Bob and Dave which is very active and he is a regular attender. He takes part in all activities held at the school on Tuesday nights and goes to Church on Sunday morning. Other events are often arranged on weekends.

Printed monthly programmes are issued to all three children to tell them exactly what is happening each week.

A few months ago, Jane appeared on the scene to care for the needs of female population. This was an invaluable move by the project co-ordinators and essential to the expansion of the project.

This now meant that different aspects could be catered for, i.e. a womens' group was formed, of which I became an active member.

There are 10 regular members but the group welcomes anyone who is interested in coming from the Edgetown area. Strong views are expressed on a wide range of subjects. We have had guest

speakers and demonstrations. Outings have been arranged and
regular visits are made to the local Sports Centre.

Charles, my 14-year-old son, has had many problems. Dave has
adopted him, unofficially, as one of his proteges. He takes him to
the Senior Club on a regular basis and encourages him to partake
in all activities. He tries to help him with his school attendance
which is very erratic. Dave does not outwardly acknowledge to
Charles that he is helping him but tries continually to gain his
confidence.

Charles has had problems with his stepfather, probably resultant from the fact that his elder brother Mark also does not get on
with him. Dave does not lay down the law but tries to lead Charles
and his friends on the right path. The work he does in this direction
is very valuable.

I have tried to outline the project as I see it, regarding the
basic obvious needs it fulfils, but I believe there is a deeper and
more unobtrusive role that it plays.

There are a lot of families in Edgetown with one problem or
another, maybe it's a son or a daughter in trouble or maybe
conflicts within the home, some are one-parent families and some
are elderly with no family. This shows a broad cross-section of
any average community. The people who run the project namely,
Bob, Dave and Jane, are special people chosen to do a special job
and they all act far beyond the call of duty, putting in endless
hours caring for the community, helping where they can, i.e.
fetching a prescription for a sick child.

The main problem in running the project seems to be in not
having any premises. Activities are spread about in any building
available. There is no lack of support for any event or activity that
is arranged, but it really would be the 'icing on the cake' if a building
was permanently available to house all the various clubs, etc.

Bob, his wife Annette, and their children, Ruth and Dave suffer
without complaint their home being used as a meeting place for
our mothers group, chess club, etc.

Edgetown without the project? Disaster, nothing, absolutely
nothing would be organized. Children would aimlessly roam the
streets, families would go wanting for support.

Bob, Dave and Jane are looked on as pillars, there when needed,
to be leaned on and often used! Solid but flexible, always willing
to listen or help.
I believe the full benefit of the project would only be felt if it
failed to exist. It is often taken for granted by both children and
parents.

(Mrs Watts)

Club Activities

On Monday 13th Feb. I had to help out at Edgetown Youth Club (junior). Tom Stephenson is a new member of the club and when Tom turned up he was too early for club and helped us set up. When club was in full swing Alan Room played table tennis with John Hillman. Trouble broke when the girls started throwing water around. We got the club running and all was going all right. Bob and Dave settled down and Wynn ran the shop.

We are friendly with police officers round our way. We have a friendly police constable, he done the beat round our way for a long time. He turned up at the club.

As the club grew to an end we started going outside for a half hour. When the little kids started coming out we had a snowball fight. Me and Tom were up against Don, Ern, Melvyn and Alice. We started in the street and ended up the other side of the church.

The Senior Youth Club was taken down to the Sports Centre for the boys and girls. There was five-a-side football for just the boys. The swimming started about 7.00 for the girls and boys. We picked up teams of five. We had a league and we played about four games each.

On Wednesday, Bob and Dave and Wynn ran a film for Edgetown Youth Club. Edgetown Youth Club (senior) got first priority for the tickets but Edgetown Youth Club (junior) got the odd tickets which can't be sold.

The films are part of the Youth Office Work they go round club to club not only our club. The film was a war film called *Where Eagles Dare.* The films are at the RC Church. My personal thoughts of the film was a very exciting film with a lot of action and very good acting and very good filming. I do not think that the girls from Junior Club enjoyed the film because they were making a lot of noise. Bob asked Wynn to run a tuck shop at the film. There is only one thing wrong with the clubs is that it's the same old faces at all the clubs run in Edgetown.

(Aston)

Some of the Wiley Group members were privileged to try their hand at para-ascending, or attempt to try — as Mick demonstrated by unfortunately being caught in a crosswind which dragged him to a barbed wire topped fence. One part of the parachute was shredded to pieces but Mick, unhurt, did eventually take to the air with the help of a new parachute.

No one was discouraged by Mick's experience and to prove that even invalids could participate, Adam (who could not be launched by a run because of a broken foot) was dragged on his stomach by a rope attached to a land rover.

All who participated thoroughly enjoyed it, it was great fun.

(Donna)

In September, 21 of us went to Butlins to a place called Filey. We went by car which took about 5 hours. We stopped twice, once on the motorway and once in a small town.

When we arrived, the chalets did not look much outside, but were good inside with 2 bedrooms and TV. I did not know who was going to do the cooking. We just took it in turns as it came.

Butlins wasn't bad. It had a fun fair, but it wasn't open all the time so we did a lot of trips to Scarborough, Filey, York and Bridlington. We had quite a bit of fun at these places, especially on the boats, speed boat, motor boat and rowing boat. I did not think we would stay upright in the rowing boat.

At the camp, we could watch TV and do odd things. One time, we went to a meeting where Roy Castle played a lot of instruments, bag pipes, a horn from Switzerland and did tap dancing. Two girls got chucked in the swimming pool. I went swimming quite a few times, sometimes in the swimming pool and once in the sea, fully clothed.

I think it is a good thing for youth clubs to get together and go places, not necessarily to Butlins, but anywhere so they can get closer together with their mates and social workers.

(Adam)

Thrown Out of the Tech College

On Wednesday, I went down to the technical college to do a catering course which I have been on for about six weeks now.

On the Wednesdays we usually have a man teacher and he is a very good teacher, and if we forget our aprons he understands, and just forgets about it. But on the particular week we had a woman to take us and she was very moany. When she came to me she told me to take my coat off and I refused. Just as I told her I would not a teacher from our school came in and asked me why I would not take my coat off and I said because I don't feel very well. Then the woman said if you don't take it off I will have to make you go back to school and the teachers said what's your choice and I said I'll stay and take my coat off.

We started preparing to do some cooking. As I started weighing out the flour I said to the boy next to me as a joke that I would beat him up and as I said that there was a teacher in front of me, and he said what did you say you would do, beat her up, and he thought that I meant the woman that was taking our class, and then he said stop looking at me like that, and he said that he would kick me out so I said that I would save him the energy and I left and as I left he asked my name and I said that I haven't got one, and I left.

As I was walking around by the tech I met my teacher and I told what had happened. So we went up to Bob's house to sort it out, and we decided that I would stay with Bob in the morning, and go back to school in the afternoon.

(Wynn)

Other Contributions

I would like to say a few words about our long-suffering guinea pigs Heracles and Iphigenia. They patiently endure being blasted with cold air everytime the back door opens. They nobly tolerate having youth club equipment dumped on their hutches and imperturbably turn not a hair when names of varying degree of insult are hurled at them by members of the family to get it off their chests. Both of them placidly munch their hay while little boys threaten to chop them up, make guinea-pig pie or send them to various horrific fates (usually described in lurid detail).

The offspring of this pair of guinea pigs have provided much pleasure to the children on the estate who would troop down daily to visit them and maybe, later, own them.

All in all, I would say the guinea pigs have contributed greatly to the project, not least because they keep me, my brother and everybody else sane. King George may have talked to trees but people in our house talk to the guinea pigs, who are available day and night and don't answer back.

(Ruth)

I myself am in the hands of Dave. If it had not been for Dave I would have lost my flat and everything else, I used to drink all my money away and if it was not for Dave Wiles who took my order books and cheque book away from me I would have been out on the streets as where I was before I moved. I now attend the church but I am not an active member. I would just like to say thank you for taking a hold of me and making me see what life was really all about.

(Roy)

A book about Edgetown? Why not? Certainly with an area as

complex as this southwestern edge, it would merit more than a few episodes of peak viewing on the box.

We can thank God for the Edgetown Project. Football, table tennis, play schemes, youth club, rounders, Jucos, encompassing all ages in the community. When people relax together troubles are shared and trust is deepened. People who care help those in need and in turn many who receive aid, themselves give in gratitude. The good, so often buried beneath the cares a sick society has imposed, comes to the surface and then something better and healthier is nurtured for the benefit of all.

There must be frustrations and disappointments in plenty for the leaders of the project and I pray that Bob, Dave and Jane together with many helpers will be allowed to continue.

(Fay)

9   To Be Continued

'The kids are great'

Edgetown is not the grossly socially deprived, overcrowded inner city. Having lived in Birmingham and Glasgow, I know there is no comparison between their crumbling Victorian bleakness and the compact council houses of Edgetown. Edgetown is just a small, pre-war, local authority estate situated on the borders of a modestly sized town. True, it lacks amenities and scores high on certain indices in relation to much of the rest of the city. But it is probably similar to thousands of other council estates. It must be remembered that, in terms of quantity, most crimes, most poverty, most social handicaps, occur outside of what are known as 'socially deprived areas' even though they occur in greatest concentration in such places.[23] It follows that there is some sense in assessing what a child care community project can do on an estate which has its share of problems but which may be typical of many neighbourhoods elsewhere.

FAILURE AND SUCCESS

The time has come to do that assessment. The main aims of the project were to attempt to prevent children being received into public care, to help delinquents and to provide youth facilities. Success or failure?

Limitations
Three years' experience serves to underline the limitations of what a tin-pot outfit can do. Some months ago, I visited a

family to ask if their sons could wear plimsolls at club. I never bothered. As I entered, the wife handed me an eviction notice and a bailiff's warrant to remove the cooker. The husband shouted that rather than let the kids—including a six-month old baby—go without a cooker, he would break into the meter for money. Crushed into their living room, I looked into the despair and anger on the boys' faces and wondered if I would soon be dealing with their delinquency. I felt so useless against the low incomes, unemployment and overcrowding which can grind families into the ground. Against personal problems arising from structural deprivations, the project is like putting band-aid on cancer.

Apart from these structural handicaps, the project still had organizational limitations. Dave and I never coped with the social needs of girls in the area. We failed to develop parents' groups. And, at the end of three years, the project still lacked what a number of local people were asking for—a permanent building.

The Figures

Given these limitations, did the project have any influence on the number of youngsters dealt with by court orders? Table 8 allows consideration to be directed at supervision orders made by the juvenile court. In the three years preceding the project, 16.2 per cent of the orders made in the city applied to youngsters in Edgetown. This proportion occurred despite the fact that Edgetown is one of the smallest of the city's 17 wards consisting of just 24 roads. During the following three years, the initial years of the project, the percentage fell down to 14.8 per cent. Small though the ward was, the project did not work with the whole district. Thus, of the 15 orders made against Edgetown youngsters, only five concerned

Table 8
Supervision orders in city and Edgetown

	City	Edgetown	
	No.	No.	%
1973–76	74	12	16.2
1976–79	101	15	14.8

Table 9
Care orders in city and Edgetown

	City No.	Edgetown No.	%
1973—76	43	8	18.6
1976—79	39	2	5.1

those with whom we were in regular contact. Subsequently, we did meet some of the others, having learned that they had been in trouble.

Supervision orders do not entail removing children from home. Care orders can do so. Table 9 reveals that, in 1973— 76, 18.6 per cent of the city's care orders were made against Edgetown youngsters. The years 1976—79 saw a drop to 5.1 per cent. In fact the number in Edgetown declined from eight orders to two. Of these, one boy was committed almost immediately after moving to Edgetown, the other was one with whom we had been attempting to help. Both were subsequently returned home and are still there at the time of writing. If the project did prevent a handful of youngsters being sent away then obviously it saved the local authority the tens of thousands of pounds associated with costly institutional and statutory care. More important, it may have facilitated the development of more stable and more happy lives.

Supervision and care orders are options open to the courts for use against juveniles. Local authorities may also intervene into children's lives without recourse to the courts. In particular, children can be received into public care with the consent of their parents under what is called Section 1, referring to Section 1 of the Children Act (1948).[24] Such cases frequently apply to parents who cannot cope for short or long periods and often do not involve juvenile delinquency. Unfortunately, a detailed breakdown according to wards was not available from the local authority's records. However, it can be said that none of the families with whom the project worked in Edgetown had children received into care during the three years, although during this period over 80 children were annually received in the city as a whole. The one exception (referred to in Chapter 4) concerned a woman who moved to another estate but with whom I continued to work. Her two small children were temporarily placed in foster homes.

On the surface, the figures, small though they are, do indicate a promising trend. Only two boys were taken from their homes by care orders in the three years from a district which had long featured high in the city's delinquency and referral league tables. Even these two were soon restored. However, a number of qualifications must be added.

Firstly, the prevention of separations does not mean that delinquency has abated. Thus between January 1977 and October 1979, 103 juvenile crimes were recorded in Edgetown. This figure takes no account of unrecorded, unreported or non-detected crimes. Although the number suggests some reduction over previous periods it is clear that delinquency still thrives. This fact is brought home to us by the number of times we have attended court with youngsters. If our interpretation is correct, we may prevent custodial sentences by reducing—but not abolishing—the number of offences committed by certain youngsters and, when they do go to court, by explaining to magistrates the circumstances surrounding their lives.

Secondly, any preventive successes in Edgetown cannot necessarily be attributed to the project. They might be the result of teachers concentrating on certain 'at risk' children or of the local policeman successfully warning them.

Thirdly, a study which compares one ward in the city with its other wards is not taking possible demographic factors into account Possibly the proportion of the population aged 5—17 years fell in Edgetown compared with the other wards. If so,Edgetown would have had proportionately fewer youngsters liable to delinquency and family break-ups. As far as could be ascertained such differences did not develop, but the statistical material available cannot be considered completely adequate.

In order to be methodologically sound, a sophisticated research programme would have been necessary. It would have considered all forms of intervention influencing youngsters in Edgetown and the rest of the city and have isolated them from the effects of the project. Obviously, on a very small budget, refinement of this nature was not possible. Even so, the figures do stand and serve to support, if not to prove, the contention that the project had some positive outcomes in its initial years.

Some Incidents

Whatever the meaning of figures, some of the youngsters and parents themselves are convinced that the project has been of value to them. Already, in chapter 3 and 4, some examples were cited which may have given rise to their views. For instance, in the incident where Mr Sparrow went into hospital, our intervention was designed specifically to stop the children going into care. Again, when Marlene came round asking to be removed from home and hinting that she would run off with an older man, our efforts were directed at reconciling her with her mother. On another evening, 14-year-old Saul arrived on the doorstep. Already dabbling in truancy and theft, he was having battles with his father. Eventually, dad inflicted a good hiding and told Saul to clear out. Saul determined to run away but eventually came to me. We sat down on the settee and he poured out his hate for his father. Suddenly, he broke down in tears. I asked him to tell me about his parents' good points as well. Later, after phoning his dad, I took him back home.

The above incidents concerned relationships within families. The next are about youngsters who were in danger of losing their freedom because of delinquency. A boy, already having appeared in court a number of times, was trying car doors down our street. He came to one which opened and hovered between taking it or not. Seeing our house, he ran in and asked if he could sit with me until he felt stronger. Another boy agreed to meet two friends to steal a moped. At the appointed hour, he felt he couldn't face telling them he did not want to go and instead called and stayed with me. Another time, Aston and his mate knocked to say they were on the brink of theft and wanted help. Once I heard on the grapevine that two lads were planning a job. I found and stopped them just as they were starting. These, and similar incidents, do not miraculously remove the delinquent tendency but the reduction of a few offences can make the difference between being sent away and staying in the community.

Some Boys

Looking back at the youngsters with whom we had regular contact, I think of four who might well have been removed from their homes but for the project's intervention. The judgement is a subjective one but is shared by Dave, by the teachers involved, and by the boys themselves. Aston's truancy would probably have got so out of hand as to make statutory action inevitable. Wynn, Adam and Kent were so into delinquency that further court appearances would probably have resulted in custodial sentences. Of course, they are still in Edgetown and may yet find themselves removed.

The project does not claim to change personalities. Hopefully, it diverts vulnerable youngsters away from truancy and delinquency during their years of 10–17 and so prevents them being dragged into a penal system which can mar their whole lives.

Attention has been focused on those youngsters whose behaviour was an obvious problem. Our involvement with other boys and girls was less dramatic but perhaps just as valuable. Relieving boredom, being a father-figure, acting as a counsellor and friend, implied giving services which they both needed and desired. Possibly, too, our interaction with adults, with children and with the community as a whole may have strengthened parents in coping with their youngsters.

Facilities

The project did succeed in supplying youth amenities where previously none existed. In any week in term time around 200 children made use of them. The clubs did hold the interest of a number of delinquent members and provided some relief from boredom. All was achieved at an annual cost of less than the salaries of three field social workers in a London borough! The existence of such facilities in themselves almost justifies the existence of the project. For my personal view is that Edgetown children have as much right to clubs, groups, outings, holidays, play schemes and sporting activities as do the more affluent members of our society.

Local Approval
Dave and I were agreed that we had no justification for staying
unless local residents valued and wanted the project. By door-
knocking, by responses to the project newspaper and by
street-corner conversation, we attempted to guage opinions.
Criticisms were made, occasional hostility was met. We were
accused of having favourites, of helping some families but not
others, of being 'too soft' with some youngsters. But the overwhelming view of both adults and children appeared to be
that they wanted us to continue.

MORE PROJECTS?

If the Edgetown project contains signs that it is partially
achieving its objectives, then considerations might be given to
creating more on the same lines.

Essential Features
What are its basic features which would have to be incorporated
into new schemes? The foregoing narrative suggests they are
fourfold. First, availability. Residents have been able to find
the project when in need. One morning, a woman contacted
me to complain that her teenage son had barricaded himself
in the loft and would not go to school. Within minutes, I was
tight-rope walking on the bannisters in order to push the trap
door (and boy on it) to one side. He was in some trouble at
school and was too frightened to attend. I accompanied him,
explained the reasons to his teacher and by 9.30 a.m. the
matter was closed. The ingredients were that the woman
knew where to find me, that she could do so quickly and that
I already knew the boy. In combination with my living nearby,
they constituted availability.

Second, tuned-in locally. The area on which we intially
concentrated contained under 500 houses, probably less than
1,500 people. As time went by, youngsters were attracted
from streets outside this core but it still remained such a small
locality that we came to know it intimately. Walking the
streets, gossiping at doors, getting to know families, became
the means by which needs were identified and helpers

recruited. The shopkeeper knew me well enough to lean over the counter to inform me of a rumour that a young child was being given drugs by her parents. A lady was confident enough to stop me in the shop with a query about adoption. I met an elderly woman in the street, fell into conversation and discovered that she was bringing up her six-year-old grandson, the parents having split up and departed. Thereafter, she was delighted to bring the child to our activities. Moreover, the same closeness that gave access to local needs also became the avenue to recruiting local help. Perhaps the major strength of the project was the involvement of Dave Wiles, Helen, the mums and teenagers in running the clubs and other activities.

Third, the ordinary and the extra-ordinary. The clubs, the football teams, the community activities provided facilities for some people who had no need of social workers. None the less, this approach was essential in securing local approval for the project. Further, the activities came to constitute a range of services which could be offered to those with problems expressed as truancy, delinquency or coping with children. Not least, the broad approach meant that people coming to the house were not thereby labelled as having a social work problem.

Fourth, administrative flexibility. The Church of England Children's Society was confident enough to loosen the project from its normal bureaucracy. Consequently, we were free to choose a small neighbourhood on which to concentrate, to run community youth clubs in ways not previously undertaken by the Society, to decide our own hours of work and what records to keep. The upshot was that we preserved our energies for the needs and demands which we considered most relevant to the project's objectives.

Local Authorities

In Britain, local authorities are the main instruments for conveying the personal social services. In the narrative, I have sometimes stressed the advantages of the community social work approach against statutory social work as I experienced it. But the question must now be asked, could local authorities incorporate the above features and so run community child care projects themselves? Of course, it might be argued that they already do so. Certainly, a number of council social workers live in the areas where they work while a few Social Services Departments have founded Family Advice Centres in areas of high need.[25] However, to my knowledge, councils have not funded employees to use their homes as their base. Even if they have, this book may constitute a pressure to multiply such experiments.

On the other hand, it could be objected that local authorities do not possess the powers to run projects of this kind that, as I have pointed out, their social workers are frequently too overburdened with their many statutory duties, and that the size of the geographical areas covered by social work teams is far too large for a community approach.

The Children and Young Persons Act (1963) placed a duty on local authorities to diminish 'the need to receive children into or keep them in care . . . or to bring children before a juvenile court'. Subsequently, councils not only undertook preventive work with so called 'at risk' youngsters in their own homes but, in the case of Family Advice Centres, covered a spectrum that included children not classified as 'at risk'. It seems that local authorities do possess the powers to run community child care projects and hence have the scope to incorporate the *ordinary and extra-ordinary* feature. Further, the study already referred to, *Social Service Teams: The Practitioners View*, makes it clear that local authorities vary in the distribution of tasks placed on individual social workers. *Flexibility* in the sense of being freed from the normal round of duties is a possibility. Moreover, recent investigations have examined the development of 'patch systems' by a few Social Services Departments. The system is defined as teams 'functioning . . . from a small geographical base and with community orientated methods of working'.[26] The authors describe five patches varying in size from 4,500 to 20,000 residents with the teams including not just social workers but also home helps, social work assistants or domiciliary care organizers. Notably, the teams found that working in smaller-than-usual areas 'made the teams more accessible and more acceptable in the eyes of their clientele'. Although not commonplace, these experiments do show that local authorities do possess the capacity to be *tuned-in locally*.

The patch system is not identical to a community child care project. None the less, there seems to be no legal barrier to local authorities concentrating on very small areas and adopting the same form of *availability*. Thus, it would be possible for them to run schemes which included the four features essential to community child care.

I am not suggesting that all Social Services Departments appoint workers of the kind described in this book. The proposal is that some should experiment with appointments both on estates like Edgetown and on the even harder inner ring areas and huge council estates of large cities. Preferably, the workers would reside in and work from their homes, have access to community buildings, be freed from normal statutory duties and relate closely to other social and community workers in the area teams. Alternatively, local authorities might fund national voluntary societies to administer the projects. Or again, they could finance local community groups to employ their own community social workers. Possibly, the latter two organizations might have greater appeal in recruiting local help.

The extension of community child care approaches under the wing of statutory bodies would raise other questions such as whether workers would feel obliged to report juvenile offences, to what extent they could side with local residents against council decisions and so on. The present narrative has concentrated on what one small voluntary outfit can and cannot do, so space can not be devoted to a discussion of these issues. But one other point must be mentioned—cash. The 1980s is not a propitious time to advocate more council expenditure. Whether authorities decide to back community child care must depend on what value they place upon it and whether they are prepared to finance prevention now in order to make future savings. These savings refer not just to the financial economy of not spending on institutional care but also to the greater personal happiness and more positive development usually associated with children staying in their own homes and communities. It is worth adding, that the costs of the Edgetown project have not been high, amounting to little more than two modest salaries, part-time secretarial assistance, transport costs and a few hundred pounds for halls and equipment.

The Skills Required

Having agencies prepared to back community child care projects is not sufficient. They will also require community social workers with suitable skills. While not claiming to possess them to any great degree, it may be useful to list the skills which we found most useful or which we wished we had possessed.

First, community skills. Skill is perhaps the wrong term to describe the rapport, the banter, the outgoing readiness to relate to a neighbourhood. This general attitude becomes more specific once door-knocking is undertaken as a means both of introducing the project and of identifying local needs. Once needs are established and local support secured, workers use their capacity to secure resources, to find premises, to raise money.

Second, youth work skills. The Edgetown Project developed a youth perspective which operated in groups and in clubs. These activities meant having to plan programmes, keep control, stimulate craft work, go camping, canoeing and swimming. Sometimes a qualification as a football referee or film projectionist seemed more desireable than a diploma in social work.

Third couselling skills. As explained, we were not capable of offering therapy. We were content with what we termed 'counselling'. Much time with individuals was given over to listening, comforting and guiding. At times, we were talking with adults about difficulties in their marriages or about their ability to control their children. At other times, we conversed with youngsters about their crimes, their sadness at not having two parents or their anger when all the odds seemed loaded against them. It was while dealing with fears, pain, separations and anger that my own training in social work was most relevant. Interestingly, however, Dave Wiles also learned to meet these emotional demands.

Fourth, advisory and negotiating skills. Often we could advise residents because we possessed more knowledge about social security, divorce, custody or maintenance. Sometimes the advice had to be transferred into negotiations with officials either on behalf of or in company with residents.

Fifth, co-operative skills. Considerable time was spent co-operating with other agencies. Thus in the year 1977–78, I had contact with 30 different agencies and met 61 of their employees. These included education welfare officers, health visitors, ministers, policemen, social security officials, probation officers, councillors, doctors, teachers and housing officers. In particular, I liased with 10 social workers from the local Social Services Department. Such contacts were essential both for agreeing on our approaches to individuals and for securing resources for local people.

Sixth, practical skills. Such as a readiness to make five-a-side football goals, to repair the snooker table and to maintain the sports gear. Not that we were very proficient. I wish that I had been knowledgeable about mending motorbikes—that would have been a great point of contact with local lads.

Skills are necessary but not sufficient. In community social work, they have to be allied with commitment, commitment to work at all hours, to endure when the going is hard. I have been stretched to my limits in this job and do not think I could survive if the demands became much greater. Yet I hope this kind of project will be tested in even tougher areas. It will require people with skills, commitment, stability and emotional and physical strength. Such people are around and hopefully agencies will be prepared to provide them with the financial and administrative backing so that their personal resources can be used to work with youngsters in their communities.

POLITICAL OBSERVATIONS

Edgetown estate does not exist in a vacuum. One danger of concentrating on a small project is that sight is lost of the relationship between the estate, the city and society as a whole. The relationship is partly a political one in which the estate and its residents appear at a disadvantage. Over the last three years, having observed the disadvantage at first hand, I have often been left with a sense of anger. In some ways I am reluctant to record my observations for there will be some readers who will have sympathized with the preventive work of the project but who will be offended by the political implications which I make. But make them I must for I believe

the material and social disadvantages experienced by residents
are at odds with the political and Christian beliefs which I hold.

Inequalities
Some Edgetown families are comfortably off. They receive
average incomes and have few or no dependent children.
Others are not so fortunate. I know of a large family which
gets through the week by borrowing from me. I know families
who are clothed from jumble sales. I know homes where the
money and food may run out before the week is up. Living
on a low wage or social security can mean perpetual anxiety
while a miscalculation or an unexpected bill can spell disaster.
Then I read of the affluent with five-figure incomes, with
second homes and expensive company perks. Both the deprived
and the privileged may be minorities but I can see no justification for the perpetuation of either if it is accepted that the
earth was created for the benefit of all, not just for a few.

As well as income inequality, I have observed inequality
before the law. A lone mother cheated social security of £10.
The offence was discovered and I encouraged her to tell the
truth. She offered to repay the money. I asked the officials if
they would accept the cash and forgo prosecution. They
insisted on a court appearance with the result that she suffered
a fine and her name in the paper. By contrast, in the same
period, I read that the government decided not to prosecute
the traitor Anthony Blunt. Again, I know a man with four
small children and no money who broke into his meter to
steal a few pounds. He was jailed for six months. By contrast,
I read of an aristocrat receiving a suspended sentence after
obtaining £13,000 by false pretences. These are selected
instances, not necessarily typical ones. But their extremes
may help to explain why lower-working-class youngsters and
adults are more liable to prosecution and custodial care than
other sections of society.

These inequalities matter. The community social worker
faces the results every day. Wilson and Herbert summed up
their classic research thus, 'in the final analysis the problem
of disadvantaged children does not lie in the genetic or
psychological deficits, it lies in the unequal distribution of
the resources of our society.'[27]

Families at the wrong end of inequality, those with low incomes, are faced with such disadvantages. The resultant diffculties they face in bringing up their children mean that the latter become more liable to delinquency or being received into public care. Of course, the abolition of poverty, the reduction of extreme inequalities, would not lead to the end of delinquency, truancy and family separations. As explained in chapter 2, other explanations of these problems point to biological, family and environmental causes which would still remain. I believe that some individuals will commit offences in any situation—just as others will always commit the sins of pride, jealousy and immorality. None the less, I also believe that greater equality—not equality for that is impossible— would mean fewer people experiencing those social depriva- tions which inhibit good child rearing methods: fewer young- sters suffering the educational handicaps which precipitate truancy; fewer kids being propelled into a boredom and resentfulness which ends in crime; fewer families being subjected to the strains so severe that eventually they crack. Above all, my faith is that a more equal society would be less split by the envy, suspicion and fear which are the food of social malaises.

Council Estate

Edgetown must also be regarded as part of the city on whose edge it is located. A quarter of all houses in the city are council dwellings, although the estates are not easily seen from the city centre. The estates and the centre make a contrast. Little public money is spent on providing amenities for Edgetown. If residents want a day nursery, swimming pool, sports facilities, a cafe, a choice of shops or a bank then they must take a bus ride—usually to the city centre. Unfor- tunatley, the bus service is extremely expensive and not frequent. Council policy appears to be to concentrate on the city centre. Cash is available to spend on floodlighting central buildings, installing new heating systems in its buildings, extending the sports complex and on publicity to attract shoppers to the city. Such public spending has occurred even at a time of economic cutbacks, when the council is reducing expenditure on council house repairs and maintenance. Clearly, the rationale behind the policy is that the city needs to trade in order to grow economically. Political issues are implicit. Would it be more advantageous to attract shops and jobs to the estate? Should a greater proportion of revenue be set aside for amenities on the estates rather than the middle of the city? If Edgetown had better facilities, then the boredom of its youngsters and the feelings of isolation of its adults would not be so apparent.

The Project's Role?

The problem of inequality, whether within a society as a whole or within one city, will require political solutions. What part can or should a community child care project play? Very little. The project cannot align itself with any one political party. It exists to serve local residents whatever their political beliefs or lack of them. Still, its workers can function in three directions. In conversations with residents we can help to define what is political. Parents often complain about the cost of living, the struggle to survive, their treatment at the hands of authority, the neglect of the estate. We could urge them just to accept their position but Dave and I feel free sometimes to discuss how conditions could or should be changed. For instance, one evening we sat in the kitchen discussing delinquency with half a dozen teenagers. Some justified theft on the grounds that they had little, while others had plenty. We pointed out that there were other more legitimate ways of redistributing money. As well as theft, we talked about career prospects, gambling and the possibility of change in the long run through political action.

Next the project workers can initiate groups with common interests. It is possible to envisage the development of gatherings concerned about day care, local play amenities or improved housing services and so on. They could exist independently of the project in order to take collective action.

Not least, we can join political parties as individuals. As a resident of Edgetown—not as a project employee—I have felt as free to identify with a local political organization as I have to align with the local church. Within ward meetings, I can speak on and make proposals for political action. Observing my allegiance, some residents, especially teenagers, have initiated political discussions and I encourage them to pursue an active role.

We can try to show that many current difficulties are really political issues. We can encourage people to become politically involved. But the project's primary objectives have a social work rather than a political edge. Moreover, the political changes to reduce inequalities will take many years—if ever—to achieve. The Edgetown Project must try to offer immediate help, no matter how limited. In some cases, problems exist which are quite unrelated to political factors, as with a youngster whose parents' inability to control him would exist in any conditions. In other cases, they occur because political policies mean that some families are too handicapped by social deprivations or the area too lacking in amenities. In either case, the Edgetown Project must act now to provide counselling and friendship for individuals and recreational facilities for the locality.

TO BE CONTINUED

The trial three years ended in the autumn of 1979. The Church of England Children's Society was then ready to accept financial responsibility for the future. Local parents and children approved and so we resolved to continue.

What is likely to happen in the future? The project needs a modest building of its own. The local authority had planned to erect another council estate next to Edgetown and within this to set aside a plot of land for the project. The site was ideal, being between Edgetown and a large post-war estate and also very near to our house. The timing of the new estate —1980. Perfect. We began to make plans to raise money, local parents talked of helping to build it themselves. Then came the cuts. The new estate was postponed. The latest unconfirmed news is that the site is to be sold to private developers. The change of plans is being opposed politically but prospects are dim.

But the project is not a building. It is people. Edgetown Project depends on the commitment of its workers and the support of residents. Dave Wiles has recently married. Consequently, he has moved out of our house into a flat in the city. We did ponder whether to approach the council to house him in Edgetown but concluded that he should not queue jump ahead of hundreds of others on the council housing list. He continues to work with the project and hopes eventually to obtain a home in the neighbourhood. Jane Thomas, is travelling in from the other side of town but is negotiating to buy a house near to Edgetown. Since her arrival, activities with girls and parents have multiplied. The mothers' group is very vocal and engages us in active debate about the directions in which the project is moving. I also want to stay. We feel we are growing with the area. Of course, as one of the youngsters so aptly put it, 'Bob's not all that young any more.' This probably explains why I now lose so many table-tennis matches and, as the team goalie, now let in about five goals a match. The physical demands are many. Perhaps the project leadership should soon be taken over by a younger person, but I hope to remain a part of it.

We do not advocate increasing the number of full-time staff. Future development, we hope, will be in terms of paying local parents for the responsibilities they are taking on within the neighbourhood. Similarly, we are trying to raise money to pay those older teenagers who help at the clubs. Hopefully, they will identify closely with the objectives of the project and be involved in its planning and decision-making.

What of the youngsters we have described in this book? A couple have married. Two have joined the armed forces. One older lad received a short prison sentence. But we are still in regular touch with nearly all. Wynn is calling regularly. Adam has settled at work. Kent wants a change from his labouring job. We are still striving to keep Aston at school. Dave and I are also seeing much more of another wave of 13–14 year olds whom we have come to know through the clubs. More teenage girls drop in to see Jane.

Despite all the difficulties experienced, we go along with the person cited in the last chapter as saying, 'The kids there are great.' Perhaps the project can work with them for the good of Edgetown. They are the future.

Notes

1   The Magistrates' Association, Association of Metropolitan Authorities and the Association of County Councils, *The Children and Young
Persons Act 1969*, October 1978, p.4.

2   In the original proposals, a number of alternative aims were listed
with the rider that they would be narrowed down as time progressed.
The original list was:
  (a)   To identify the child care needs of the neighbourhood.
  (b)   To work with parents and children in danger of being separated
        from each other. (Of course, it was accepted that, at times, the
        best outcome is for separation to occur.)
  (c)   To work with private foster parents and daily minders.
  (d)   To identify local persons who could be encouraged to help
        children in need.
  (e)   To work directly with youngsters whose delinquency was
        endangering their prospects of remaining at home.
Within a few weeks, it became clear that the area contained very few
foster parents and daily minders. Simultaneously, the lack of amenities
on the estate was concluded to be a major need relevant to preventive
work. Consequently, the project's aims were clarified and shortened to
the three given in the text.

3   Since these figures were issued, the ward boundaries have been re-
drawn and Edgetown is now more precisely in a single ward. Unfortunately, this redrawing has made more difficult the collection of data
about the area.

4   Personal communication from the councillor.

5   See my contribution to J. Stott (ed.), *Crime and the Responsible
Society*, Hodders, 1980; and R. Holman, *Poverty: Explanations of
Social Deprivation*, Martin Robertson, 1978; and R. Holman, *Child
Care and Inequality*, Child Poverty Action Group, 1976.

6   H. Wilson and G. Herbert, *Parents and Children in the Inner City*,
Routledge & Kegan Paul, 1978.

7   D. West and D. Farrington, *The Delinquent Way of Life*, Heinemann,
1977.

8   See *Community Care,* 20 September 1978, p. 19.
9   R. Priestley, D. Fears and R. Fuller, *Justice for Juveniles,* Routledge & Kegan Paul, 1977, p.49.
10   J. Packman, *Child Care: Needs and Numbers,* Allen & Unwin, 1969.
11   Despite common opinion to the contrary, the Social Tourism Study reported that most low-income families do not have a holiday away from home. Cited in *The Guardian,* 19 August 1975.
12   The diary, kept by myself, entailed noting who called at our home and the main reason for the call. Similar notes were made about the way time was spent outside the home. Obviously, this method had certain drawbacks. A person might call for several reasons and I had to assess which was the most important. Again, my memory is very fallible and my wife and colleagues are convinced that I did not record many of the calls. None the less, the diary approach did provide some quantifiable material.
   Dave Wiles also kept a diary but, of course, his recordings cover just two years, not the three of the project's initial period.
13   See M. Dean, 'Playing hookey is legal', *The Guardian,* 31 July 1979.
14   This and succeeding quotations by Dave Wiles are taken from interviews he had with a university researcher, Mr Ray Jones. Ray interviewed Dave over a period of two years in order to assess Dave's impact on the project and the effects of the work on Dave. Hopefully, the results will be published.
15   West and Farrington, *op. cit.,* p.82.
16   Department of Employment and Productivity, *Family Expenditure Survey,* HMSO, 1977.
17   D. Piachaud, *The Cost of a Child,* Child Poverty Action Group, 1979.
18   C. Bell and H. Newby, *Community Studies,* Allen & Unwin, 1971, pp. 27–32.
19   P. Parsloe, O. Stevenson *et al., Social Service Teams: The Practitioners View,* HMSO, 1978.
20   Again, Dave made this statement in an interview with Ray Jones.
21   See R. Terrill, *R.H. Tawney and His Times. Socialism as Fellowship,* Andre Deutsch, 1974.
22   The term 'professional adults' refers simply to those interviewed who had contact with Edgetown in an 'official capacity', i.e. generally all those not residents of the area, although quite coincidentally one social worker was a resident of the private housing area of Edgetown.
23   See S. Holtermann, 'Areas of urban deprivation in Great Britain: An analysis of 1971 census data', in CSO, *Social Trends,* HMSO, No.6, 1975.
24   Section 1 action can only be pursued if certain conditions are ful-

filled. For an outline of the development of child care legislation see, J. Packman, *The Child's Generation,* Basil Blackwell & Martin Robertson, 1975. Since the Child Care Act 1980, the previous Section 1 has been incorporated into the new Section 2.

25 See A. Leissner, K. Herdman and E. Davies, *Advice, Guidance and Assistance,* Longman, 1971.

26 R. Hadley and M. McGrath, 'Patched based social services', *Community Care,* 11 October 1979.

27 Wilson and Herbert, *op. cit.,* p.198.

Index